Debbie Kohler '95
Mt. Angel Abbey
May 1992

LIVING
WITH CONTRADICTION

LIVING
WITH CONTRADICTION

Reflections on
The Rule of St Benedict

Esther de Waal

1817

Harper & Row, Publishers, San Francisco

New York, Grand Rapids, Philadelphia, St. Louis
London, Singapore, Sydney, Tokyo, Toronto

For Victor

FIRST U.S. EDITION

Library of Congress Cataloging-in-Publication Data

De Waal, Esther
  [1st U.S. ed]
  Living with contradiction : reflections on the Rule of St.
 Benedict / Esther de Waal.
      p.   cm.
  ISBN 0-06-061902-3
  1. Benedict, Saint, Abbot of Monte Cassino.   Regula.
2. Monasticism and religious orders—Rules.   I. Title.
BX3004.Z5D35   1989
255'.106—dc20   89-45233
                                  CIP

89 90 91 92 93 HAD 10 9 8 7 6 5 4 3 2 1

Contents

Explanation

Early in the summer of 1988 a group of about twenty people came to spend a week together at the monastery of Holy Cross on the Hudson River in upstate New York, an Anglican monastic order which follows the Rule of St Benedict. Three months later a similar group gathered in Glastonbury, living in a retreat house overlooking the ruins of a great medieval English Benedictine abbey. Although the setting of the two was an almost total contrast, both groups shared a common aim: Benedictine Experience. This was the name given to the attempt to live out for a short space of time, and also obviously in a modified way, that way of life set out by St Benedict in his Rule. These days together were spent following that daily rhythm which is central to the Benedictine life, which recognizes that we are all made up of body, mind and spirit, that due attention must be paid to each element, that each is taken seriously, and can become a way to God. So this was neither conference, retreat, seminar nor workshop. It was simply an attempt to follow that monastic pattern which St Benedict established for his community of monks in the sixth century, but which still today continues to speak to the needs of men and women who are trying to live out their Christian life in the world.

Holy Cross and Glastonbury were only the most

recent in a succession of "Benedictine Experiences" which have been held since the idea first began in Canterbury in 1983. The original inspiration came from Canterbury itself, that great cathedral church which had throughout the Middle Ages served one of the most important Benedictine foundations of medieval Christendom. There that first summer, as we lived together in the cathedral precincts, each day was punctuated by the saying of the offices, and the eucharist; the mornings were devoted to study, and the afternoons to manual work; the evenings gave time for silence, for lectio divina (reflective reading), and a chance to relax together.

The week therefore worked at two levels. It was not only an individual experience in which each participant discovered much about him or herself through this daily balance and rhythm, it was also a shared life, an experience of making community, of learning to accept one another and to live together in love. In this it simply reflected one of the most profound insights of the Rule: unless and until we can live with ourselves, we cannot live with other people. But equally, unless and and until we have learnt to live fully and creatively with others we cannot hope to live with ourselves. So right at the outset "Benedictine Experience" faced us with a tension, the tension between the individual and the community.

The theme of the holding together of the tensions, this living with the contradictions, was the theme of the daily meditations which I gave in the summer of 1988. It is at the request of those who heard them at

Holy Cross and at Glastonbury – and not least at the request of the American Benedictine Sisters of St Benedict, St Joseph, Minnesota, where that same summer I took a retreat based on an extended exploration of this same idea – that I have written this book. My wish is that these meditations may now be read prayerfully and reflectively, just as the original meditations were designed to be heard prayerfully and reflectively. This means reading them slowly, which is not a natural accomplishment of the twentieth century, where the slow and ruminative reading familiar in an earlier age has become a rare and neglected art. It is to encourage this that they have been printed with suggestions for pauses.

They are given here very much as I originally delivered them. This means that the same themes or the same images, sometimes an actual phrase, will appear and re-appear. This is intentional. The underlying ideas surface in different contexts. This is, after all, what I find in the text of the Rule itself, it is like some closely woven tapestry, in which one is drawn first by one thread and then by another.

It is because I have come to see the Rule like a tapestry, or, to use another analogy, like some spring or source to which it is possible to return time and again, that I come back to it, making fresh demands on it, asking new questions of it, and finding that at each stage of my life and with each new step forward St Benedict points me onward and illuminates the way to God.

These meditations explore, and I hope deepen, what I was trying to do in an earlier book, *Seeking*

God, The Way of St Benedict. Then I encountered St Benedict at a time when I was an extremely busy woman – wife and mother, historian, teacher, keeping open house to countless numbers of people. That phase of my life is now past, and I find that I have more time and leisure to face questions which being so busy then had enabled me to evade. For, contrary to what I might have hoped or expected when I was younger, life does not in fact grow simpler as one gets older, its complexities and contradictions do not actually decrease as time goes on. So I turned again to St Benedict as a guide and support, to teach me to learn to live with the contradictions within myself and the world around me. My hope is that these reflections will enable others also to find in the Rule the same practical help and gentle guidance that I have found. For St Benedict is always gentle, nurturing, sensitive to each of us as individuals. There is no technology here to threaten us, no system to be acquired or mastered. Instead he will show us how to live with a series of opening doors. He shows us how to live with the contradictions; he does not tell us that they will necessarily be resolved.

In the years since I wrote *Seeking God* I have stayed in convents and monasteries on both sides of the Atlantic, and in Europe. I have found myself received as a sister in Christ by countless Benedictines. And I have also spent much time in the company of large numbers of lay people of all denominations, who are discovering that for them too the Rule can be a guide, even though they are living in the world and under no vows other than baptismal ones. What follows obviously owes much to these friendships, to time spent in praying and talking together, and to the sharing of a common life. But in the last resort this book remains simply another very personal attempt to show how the Rule continues to be mentor and inspiration on my own Christian journey. I hope that it will lead people to discover St Benedict for themselves. It is for that reason that I include at the start the Prologue to the Rule, in which all the main themes are set out, and which contains some of the most memorable passages of St Benedict's writing.

My final word of thanks must be to Heythrop College, which provided me with the place from which it was possible to write this book.

Heythrop College,
Cavendish Square,
London W1M 0AN

ESTHER DE WAAL
25th September 1988

THE RULE OF
SAINT BENEDICT

Prologue

[1]Listen carefully, my son, to the master's instructions, and attend to them with the ear of your heart. This is advice from a father who loves you; welcome it, and faithfully put it into practice. [2]The labour of obedience will bring you back to him from whom you had drifted through the sloth of disobedience. [3]This message of mine is for you, then, if you are ready to give up your own will, once and for all, and armed with the strong and noble weapons of obedience to do battle for the true King, Christ the Lord.

[4]First of all, every time you begin a good work, you must pray to him most earnestly to bring it to perfection. [5]In his goodness, he has already counted us as his sons, and therefore we should never grieve him by our evil actions. [6]With his good gifts which are in us, we must obey him at all times that he may never become the angry father who disinherits his sons, [7]Nor the dread lord, enraged by our sins, who punishes us forever as worthless servants for refusing to follow him to glory.

[8]Let us get up then, at long last, for the Scriptures

rouse us when they say: *It is high time for us to arise from sleep* (Romans 13:11). [9]Let us open our eyes to the light that comes from God, and our ears to the voice from heaven that every day calls out this charge. [10]*If you hear his voice today, do not harden your hearts* (Psalm 94 [95]:8). [11]And again: *You that have ears to hear, listen to what the Spirit says to the churches* (Revelation 2:7). [12]And what does he say? *Come and listen to me, sons; I will teach you the fear of the Lord* (Psalm 33 [34]:12). [13]*Run while you have the light* of life, *that the darkness* of death *may not overtake you* (John 12:35).

[14]Seeking his workman in a multitude of people, the Lord calls out to him and lifts his voice again: [15]*Is there anyone here who yearns for life and desires to see good days?* (Psalm 33[34]:13 [16]If you hear this and your answer is "I do," God then directs these words to you: [17]If you desire true and eternal life, *keep your tongue free from vicious talk and your lips from all deceit; turn away from evil and do good; let peace be your quest and aim* (Psalm 33[34]:14–15). [18]Once you have done this, my *eyes will be upon* you *and* my *ears will listen* for your *prayers; and even before you ask me, I will say* to you: *Here I am* (Isaiah 58:9). [19]What, dear brothers, is more delightful than this voice of the Lord calling to us? [20]See how the Lord in his love shows us the way of life. [21]Clothed then with faith and the performance of good works, let us set out on this way, with the Gospel for our guide, that we may deserve to see him *who has called* us *to his kingdom* (1 Thessalonians 2:12).

[22]If we wish to dwell in the tent of this kingdom,

we will never arrive unless we run there by doing good deeds. ²³But let us ask the Lord with the Prophet: *Who will dwell in your tent, Lord; who will find rest upon your holy mountain?* (Psalm 14[15]:1) ²⁴After this question, brothers, let us listen well to what the Lord says in reply, for he shows us the way to his tent. ²⁵*One who walks without blemish*, he says, *and is just in all his dealings;* ²⁶*who speaks the truth from his heart and has not practised deceit with his tongue;* ²⁷*who has not wronged a fellow man in any way, not listened to slanders against his neighbour* (Psalm 14[15]:2–3). ²⁸He has *foiled* the *evil one*, the devil, at every turn, flinging both him and his promptings far *from the sight* of his heart. While these temptations were still *young, he caught hold of them and dashed them against* Christ (Psalm 14[15]:4; 136[137]:9). ²⁹These people *fear the Lord*, and do not become elated over their good deeds; they judge it is the Lord working in them. ³⁰*They praise* (Psalm 14[15]:4) the Lord working in them, and say with the Prophet: *Not to us, Lord, not to us give the glory, but to your name alone* (Psalm 113[115:1]:9). ³¹In just this way Paul the Apostle refused to take credit for the power of his preaching. He declared: *By God's grace I am what I am* (I Corinthians 15:10). ³²And again he said: *He who boasts should make his boast in the Lord* (2 Corinthians 10:17). ³³That is why the Lord says in the Gospel: *Whoever hears these words of mine and does them is like a wise man who built his house upon rock;* ³⁴*the floods came and the winds blew and beat against the house, but it did not fall: it was founded on rock* (Matthew 7:24–25).

[35]With this conclusion, the Lord waits for us daily to translate into action, as we should, his holy teachings. [36]Therefore our life span has been lengthened by way of a truce, that we may amend our misdeeds. [37]As the Apostle says: *Do you not know that the patience of God is leading you to repent* (Romans 2:4)? [38]And indeed the Lord assures us in his love: *I do not wish the death of the sinner, but that he turn back to me and live* (Ezekiel 33:11).

[39]Brothers, now that we have asked the Lord who will dwell in his tent, we have heard the instruction for dwelling in it, but only if we fulfil the obligations of those who live there. [40]We must, then, prepare our hearts and bodies for the battle of holy obedience to his instructions. [41]What is not possible to us by nature, let us ask the Lord to supply by the help of his grace. [42]If we wish to reach eternal life, even as we avoid the torments of hell, [43]then – while there is still time, while we are in this body and have time to accomplish all these things by the light of life – [44]we must run and do now what will profit us for ever.

[45]Therefore we intend to establish a school for the Lord's service. [46]In drawing up its regulations, we hope to set down nothing harsh, nothing burdensome. [47]The good of all concerned, however, may prompt us to a litle strictness in order to amend faults and to safeguard love. [48]Do not be daunted immediately by fear and run away from the road that leads to salvation. It is bound to be narrow at the outset. [49]But as we progress in this way of life and in faith, we shall run on the path of God's

commandments, our hearts overflowing with the inexpressible delight of love. [50]Never swerving from his instructions, then, but faithfully observing his teaching in the monastery until death, we shall through patience share in the sufferings of Christ that we may deserve also to share in his kingdom. Amen.

I

A Way of Healing

We all stand in need of healing. We are all seeking wholeness. For most of us it is a most urgent and ever-present reality in our lives, one we may perhaps try to bury or neglect but which, if we are honest with ourselves, we find we cannot ignore. We all know also that unless we attend to our inner conflicts and contradictions, not only will we find ourselves torn apart by our inner divisions but also we shall very likely inflict wounds on those around us.

❈

Our God, the God of love, does not want a broken and divided self. He created us for fullness of life. He created each of us to be a free son or daughter, that son or daughter whom in our deepest being each of us longs to be, to become. And we all know in our heart of hearts (even if we are unwilling to admit it) that this healing of our divisions, this search for wholeness, must be an ongoing process. There is no once and for all moment when we can say that at last we are whole, the past is buried and over, the hurts forgotten, the wounds healed. Instead we find

11

that it is to be a search that we must expect to continue throughout our lives.

🙚

This search is one that is very evident in our world today. Concern for healing and for wholeness is a theme much written or spoken about. There are countless paperbacks with the word "healing" in the title. There are countless workshops which hold out the promise of healing. Faced with something which none of us can evade, even if we wanted to, I believe that we can turn to the Rule of St Benedict, and find there a handbook of healing. St Dunstan's first biographer, almost a thousand years ago, described the saint as a man "following the health-giving Rule of St Benedict". I am sure the same can be true of us all today. But the promise is not one of some idealistic, escapist healing, which will lead us into some easy wholeness. Rather the promise is that we shall learn to live with contradiction, holding together the tensions in such a way that will let them become creative and life-enhancing for us. And in fact I find it reassuring to think that there is no easy path, no short cuts, no simplistic answer.

Jean Vanier writes of this with understanding when he says

In our times there is a danger of thinking that everyone may become perfectly healed and find perfect unity in themselves and with others.

This type of idealism is rampant everywhere. New therapies engender more and better illusions. And each day new techniques are born which will bring about this long-awaited healing. Personally I am more and more convinced that there is no perfect healing. Each human being carries their own wounds, their own difficulties of relationships and their own anguishes. It is a question of learning to live day after day with this reality and not in a state of illusion . . .

❦

When we stop and look at ourselves we are broken and fragmented in so many areas of our being – in our relations not only with ourselves, but also with other people, with the world around us, and not least of all with God himself. Here are the four aspects of our lives which we must all at some time confront if we are to grow into that fullness of stature to which we are called. This search for healing is a search which is common to us all; it is basic to our humanity. We are faced with it right from the start, in the Garden of Eden. We return to that story and find there a story that is our own. For each of us is Adam and each is Eve. And as we read what happened there, step by step the full impact of those successive alienations is brought to bear on us. We see the drama unfolding in relentless detail with an almost terrifying sense of inevitability about what men and women can do to themselves.

꧁

The setting is a garden. There are two players, but dominating it all is God, his voice heard, his presence felt. We watch what happens. Encouraged by that subtle snake the man and the woman, whole in their nakedness, disobey the very simple command given to them by God. The relationship of God with the men and women of his own creating has been challenged and damaged. Then immediately they discover that they are naked, and so they sew fig leaves together to make a garment which will cover parts of themselves. Here is a split within themselves, for when they cover their nakedness with leaves they are rejecting their original wholeness. And then God speaks to Adam, and Adam blames Eve, but Eve says it was all due to the snake. Then God speaks to Adam of the enmity that there will be between him and the woman, and he speaks to Eve of the pain that she will feel in child-bearing. Now there are splits in the relations between persons. And finally God tells Adam that he is to till the earth with sweat on his brow – there is no longer any harmonious relationship with the earth. Here is the split with the environment.

꧁

All these elements are part of the drama. They tell me that I must not think that I can try to heal myself without also trying to heal my relationships with other people, those with whom I have to live. Nor must I forget that I have a debt to the world around me, to the earth and the environment that gives me life. But above all there is God himself, the root and ground of my being. Unless my relationship with him is made whole I shall remain standing in the shadow of the tree in the Garden of Eden, instead of standing under the shadow of that tree which is the cross on the hill of Calvary – the cross that speaks to me of God's forgiving and redeeming love.

❦

The cross also tells me that there are no short cuts. The wood that went to make the cross was taken from a living tree, but a tree that has been cut, shaped, transformed. The process of cutting, stripping and reshaping is never easy or comfortable; it is protracted and painful. Then the cross itself stands there, its main thrust downwards into the ground, its arms stretching outwards, a balance of two opposing forces, vertical and horizontal held together in a dynamic tension. Only so can it be life-giving. In that tension lies a most powerful image for what is at work in my own life. In that transformation I must expect to be shaped, formed and re-formed; nor can I ever hope to escape the tension that lies at the centre and makes possible the holding together of the whole.

❄

Another way of expressing this truth would be to see it in terms of a continual dying and rebirth throughout my life. That I cannot have new life without death is the most fundamental and inescapable of all the tensions I have to hold on to. Here I remind myself of what was really involved in the nativity at Bethlehem, putting aside all the popular representations that have obscured a rather harsh reality: a child laid in a hollowed stone trough, warm human flesh placed on cold, bare stone, a prefiguring – right at the moment of birth – of the moment when that same body would be laid to rest in the stone of the tomb, death and life inextricably bound together.

❄

St Anselm opens one of his prayers with the disarmingly simple words, "O God, who has formed and re-formed me . . ." As I pray them I realize that this is one of God's mercies: that he allows me to remain open, vulnerable, sensitive to the ways in which he is ready to shape and mould me; that I am indeed clay in the hands of the potter; and that continually throughout my life the old gives way to the new – if

I am willing to let it happen, if I am ready to play my part.

✠

I also realize that my own co-operation comes into play; that I must genuinely desire to move forward. My difficulty is that this desire is not always there, that often it seems so much easier and more appealing to stop, to look back, to fossilize, to refuse to grow. I also realize that I must be willing to receive, not proud and isolated, standing confident and aloof in my own self-sufficiency. Can I identify myself with those who sought out Christ in his earthly ministry, coming forward to find him and urge him to heal them? Seeking him out, waiting for him, making their way to him by themselves or with the help of friends? I can read the gospels as an account of a God of healing at work amidst the pain and suffering of the world. Certainly they make it plain that Christ walked in constant awareness of the pain of the world, as well as of its beauty and potential. He never minimized the problems of suffering and of evil. He never offered an explanation which would trivialize human anguish. But by taking human suffering seriously he took human dignity seriously. This comes over most poignantly in St Matthew's Gospel (9:35–6):

> Jesus went about all the cities and villages,
> teaching and preaching ... and healing ...
> every infirmity. When he saw the crowds he

had compassion for them, because they were
harrassed and helpless like sheep without a
shepherd.

That analogy with a shepherd is a very powerful
image. Ezekiel describes the care of the shepherd for
his flock:

> The Lord Yahweh says this: I am going to look
> after my flock myself, and keep all of it in view.
> As a shepherd keeps all his flock in view when
> he stands up in the middle of his scattered sheep
> so I shall keep my sheep in view . . . I shall look
> for the lost one, bring back the stray, bandage
> the wounded, and make the weak strong . . . I
> shall be a true shepherd to them. (Ezekiel
> 34:11–16).

"To bandage the wounded, and make the weak
strong . . .' In the Benedictine community the abbot
holds the place of Christ and plays the role of good
shepherd to the sheep. The shepherd is above all the
one who seeks, who goes after the stray, who
searches for the lost and who brings them back to
the fold. There is here something which we all
recognize. For not only are we seeking God. He is
seeking us.

> To seek God
> means first of all
> to let yourself be found by him.
> He is the God of Abraham, Isaac and Jacob.
> He is the God of Jesus Christ.
> He is your God

not because He is yours
but because you are His.
To choose God
is to realize that you are known and loved
in a way surpassing anything you can imagine
long before anyone had thought of you or spoken
  your name.

We are being sought, just as we are in all our weakness and woundedness. St Benedict writes as a man full of compassion and understanding. He expects much from all in his monastery, and yet he also recognizes that some are frail, old, sick, slow, lazy – and I may be any of these at various times in my life. He accepts this, indeed he starts from this, making concessions and allowances, building on the frailty and brokenness of our humanity. He points us a way to God which nurtures as well as challenges, which believes in our potential and yet makes sure that no more is asked of us than we can actually bear. A later Benedictine, St Anselm, writing in the twelfth century, expresses this nurturing, this gentleness in a prayer which asks

And you Jesus, are you not also a mother?
Are you not the mother who like a hen
Gathers her chickens under her wings?

St Benedict's starting point then is that Christ accepts me, just as I am now, with all my weakness and confusion, in all my complexity and contradiction. He does not want me to deny this. He does not ask me to act as though the frailty and the pain and the failure were not real. The first step for transforming that pain is to look at it with honesty, and then open myself up to God's healing and transforming love. I must not forget the pain that went into the shaping of a living tree into the cross. I must not forget that Christian discipleship is costly. Yet I hold on to the promise that ends the Prologue, that "we shall run on the path of God's commandments, our hearts overflowing with the inexpressible delight of love". It is in the certainty of that love, that total and unconditional love that makes all things possible, that we dare to move forward on the path of healing, transformation and new life.

The Power of Paradox

"A harvester of grain, borrowing from others and making one bundle out of many that had gone before." This ninth-century description of St Benedict draws a nice picture of a man open to different streams of thought.

At the very end of the Rule comes an unobtrusive small sentence which is in fact extremely illuminating. St Benedict cites for further reading, after what he claims is his own modest Rule, St Basil on the one hand and the desert fathers on the other. Now these two sources are very different in emphasis. St Basil is writing out of the experience of community living, the desert fathers out of the experience of hermit life. The former is more humane, aware of the relations between the brothers, the latter more ascetic, aware of the need for silence and solitude. In composing his Rule it is clear that St Benedict was writing in the context of the two monastic traditions into which he entered. Thus it is possible to read his text and to see its fundamental concern as the making of community; or equally to find its main interest as a life for training in silence and asceticism. Perhaps it is more valuable to make out a case for both, to recognize that St Benedict's insight was to put these two streams together and let them stimulate one another. By giving mutual respect and full acceptance to both he provides a milieu in which both kinds of monks, with their respective attractions, could live together, help one another, and, by being different, enrich one another.

In drawing from both streams he is setting up a dialogue that allows them to interact in a way that will produce growth. He avoids extremism, he is open to differing, even divergent, aspects of the truth. Differences will not be solved by pretending that they do not exist, or that only one orientation is legitimate. It is rather a question of setting limits to each so that neither takes off in its own direction to the practical destruction of the other. The result is not confusion but a holding together of polarities that leads to vitality. Here is the secret of the dynamism that the Rule can bring to the life of a community, as also to the life of an individual. The result has been that the Benedictine tradition, operating from this base, has adapted itself to new situations and has responded to new challenges throughout its history. And what is true of how it has shaped a monastic institution is also, I believe, true of how – if we are prepared to allow it – it will shape each of us as individuals.

※

This polarity, this holding together of opposites, this living with contradictions, presents us not with a closed system but with a series of open doors. This is, I suspect, the way most of us actually experience our lives. We find that we have to make room for divergent forces within us, and that there is not necessarily any resolution of the tension between them. I find it immensely liberating and encouraging to be told that this is the way things are, and that the way things are is good. St Benedict here is at his most creative and his most realistic. He describes a way of life which is immediately familiar, because it is precisely the way in which I myself live. In holding on to this polarity I must not deny the truth of either, for the two poles are not mutually antagonistic. On the contrary, each makes the other possible. St Benedict is a master of paradox.

❧

We are all people of paradox. Each of us knows only too well the conflicting claims

> of child and adult
>
> of male and female
>
> of animus and anima
>
> of heart and head.

Living with paradox may well not always be easy or comfortable. It is not something for the lazy, the complacent, the fanatical. It does however point us the way to truth and life. For as we learn to live with paradox we have to admit that two realities may be equally true; we may be asked to hold together contrasting forces. The closer we come to saying something worthwhile, the more likely it is that paradox will be the only way to express it. "The mind will never apprehend the truth of paradox. Only the heart can do that."

But if paradox speaks to my human condition it is also a vehicle for expressing truths about

> a God who becomes a man
> a victor who rides on a donkey in his hour of triumph
> a saviour who is executed like some common thief
> a king whose kingdom is not here but to come
> a God who tells me that "when I am weak then I am strong"
> a God whose promise is that "in losing my life I shall find it".

Here is a God who proclaims the ultimate paradox of life through death, a paradox which can only be lived, it cannot be explained; it can be celebrated, it cannot easily be discussed. For in the cross we are presented with the ultimate paradox. As Parker Palmer has written,

> The cross calls us to recognize that the heart of human experience is neither consistency nor

chaos, but contradiction. In our century we have been beguiled by the claim of consistency, by the theory that history is moving toward the resolution of all problems, by the false hope that comes from groundless optimism that all works together for good. And then, when this claim has been discredited by tragic events, we have been assaulted by theories of chaos, by prophets of despair who claim that everything can be reduced to the random play of forces beyond all control, of events which lack inherent meaning.

But the cross symbolizes that beyond naive hope and beyond meaningless despair lies a structure of dynamic contradictions in which our lives are caught.

The Christ on the Cross is the ultimate contradiction, holding together the vertical, pointing towards the Father, and the horizontal arms stretched out to the world. This is the Christ towards whom St Benedict is pointing
    Christ present with an eternal Yes
    Bringing light out of darkness
    Bringing life out of death.

But of course I also know that I can only too easily experience the wrong sort of contradiction in my life. I can be pulled in two directions at once so that I am fragmented and disoriented. I then become a battlefield in which contrary forces tug me first in one direction and then in another. This is the divided heart of which the psalmist speaks. This is the house divided against itself which cannot stand. This is the paralysed self which appears when the inner and the outer fail to correspond. Instead I need to try to find some degree of equilibrium and unity within myself which will allow these contradictory forces to work together, which will enable the tensions to become life-giving.

Perhaps another way of expressing this would be to say that what I am looking for is some sort of balance in my life—a balance "so delicate, so risky, so creative", as Maria Boulding puts it, that she likens it to a bird in flight, a dancer in motion. One of the favourite words in the Rule is "run". St Benedict tells me to run to Christ. If I stop for a moment and consider what is being asked of me here, and what is involved in the act of running, I think of how when I run I place first one foot and then the other on the ground, that I let go of my balance for a second and then immediately recover it again. It is risky, this matter of running. By daring to lose my balance I keep it.

Or another way of thinking about this might be to reflect on the rhythmic alternation which governs the whole of life. Throughout the Rule we are made aware of the conflicting demands of body, mind and spirit, and of the need to pay attention to their contrasting claims. There must be time to work, time to study and time to pray. There must be time to pray in solitude and time to pray with others. There must be time to be alone and time to be in community. There is a daily, weekly, yearly pattern of life in the monastery. Life is inextricably bound up in the alternation of day and night, of the changing seasons, of the ebb and flow of the seasons, of the changing shape of the liturgical year. This way of life brings us into touch with the rhythm inherent in all things, in the holding together of the contradiction of growth and decline, of light and dark, of dying and rising again.

Here is something profoundly important for my own humanity. To paraphrase what Parker Palmer has written in *The Promise of Paradox*, if I am to live wholly and fully and freely then I must accept that I am in the contradictions and that the contradictions are in me, and that all is held together by a "hidden wholeness". When I became aware of my relatedness to all of life, to the dark and to the light, to death and to life, then I can walk freely in the certainty that the ultimate contradiction of the Cross is also the promise of fullness of life.

Living with the Contradictions

The Rule of St Benedict addresses itself to us, each of us, just as we are. St Benedict understands human nature, its strengths and weaknesses, limitations and potential. He respects the mystery that each person is, and the result of this is that the thrust of the Rule is never towards dictating, rather it is towards the inner disposition of the heart. This is an approach which follows from his firm understanding that each of us is a highly complex being, and that allowance must be made for this.

When a novice enters the monastic community and lays the vows on the altar, the prayer is always *Suscipe me*, accept me, O Lord. These are wonderful words that I too can come back to, time and again, as a prayer for myself: accept me, O Lord, just as I am, in my frailty, my inadequacy, my contradictions, my confusion. Accept me in my complexity, with all those discordant currents that pull me in so many directions. Accept all of this, and help me so to live with what I am that what I am may become my way to God. Accept the tensions and help me to hold them together, so that I may learn to live fully, freely, wholly, not torn apart but finding that balance and harmony that will allow me to discover my point of inner equilibrium.

※

I suspect it is true of all of us that the older we grow the more urgent it becomes that we learn to live with these discords within ourselves, and live with them in such a way that we are neither fragmented nor exhausted; not succumbing to lassitude or depression but rather learning how to hold tensions together and let them become powers for good, powers to liberate and affirm us, powers to release the energy to allow us to run the way to God that is St Benedict's concern in the prologue to the Rule: "Run while you have the light of life . . . Run on the path of God's commandments, our hearts overflowing with the inexpressible delight of love."

What I have gained from the written text of the Rule has been made more vivid and immediate for me by the way in which the themes addressed by the Rule are reflected in Benedictine monastic buildings themselves. Living for ten years under the shadow of Canterbury cathedral has furnished me with images that have slowly worked themselves into my subconscious, have fed me and sustained me and above all coloured my understanding of the Rule and of the life to which it gives rise. Two images in particular seem illuminating. In the crypt, built in the twelfth century when St Anselm was abbot and archbishop, the massive romanesque pillars bear amazing carved capitals. The four sides of one show a succession of scenes: on the first, a carefree jester throws a fish into a bowl as he perches on another's head; on the second, a lion, an amiable creature with a curling tail, smiles an innocent, warm smile. On the third side the mood changes: here we find strange, devouring creatures that feel like elemental forces at work attempting to swallow or destroy one another. Finally, on the fourth side there is a double-headed monster combining male and female features. Here is the contradiction between the light and the dark, the masculine and the feminine, the life-enhancing and the life-destroying. This portrayal was put here, in this holy place, by men who were not afraid to carve what they knew and present it to God in the heart of their monastic crypt. I find here a very simple message that we all need to hear: being committed to God is not about being nice. It is about being real.

❧

The second image comes from the vault of the nave, built towards the end of the Middle Ages. Stand beneath that triumph of late Gothic building and you find pillar and arch, rib and vault, all brought together in one great harmonious unity, each separate and individual part linked both with the other elements and with the whole. Here is the Pauline analogy of the body of Christ spelt out in stone. Here is a statement in the structure of the church itself of that common life experienced by the medieval Benedictine community and well described in a sermon by one of its thirteenth-century abbots "Being many we are one body, members of one another. And one spirit gives life to our whole body through the members and parts, and brings about a mutual peace . . ."

But to discover the secret of this harmonious unity, this peace and concord, one has to climb the hidden stairways and explore the space between the stone vaults and the roofs above. Here is thrust and counter-thrust. Here is never-ending conflict. The high vaults strive to push the walls outwards; the flying buttresses strive to push them inwards. Here are columns, arches, walls all locked in unceasing combat. This great cathedral is maintained, and has been maintained for centuries, through the interplay and interdependence of contradictory forces, the unremitting pull of opposites.

The keystone is firm at the point of equilibrium.
The boss is still at the heart of the tensions.

❦

If there is a single reason why the Benedictine way of life has remained dynamic across the centuries, I suspect it is because the Rule carries within itself this same ability to hold together opposing forces, conflicting tensions. I believe that the Rule is able to feed the divergent streams within each of us because it is itself made up of divergent streams. It is precisely here that its fecundity lies, as does also that of my own humanity; the riches of my own make-up depend upon allowing these streams to work dynamically within me.

Living in a cave at Subiaco, St Benedict knew the solitary life of a hermit for many years before founding his community of monks at Monte Cassino. Here is something profoundly important for all of us. Unless and until I first learn to respect my own solitude, revere my own identity, recognize the mystery that I myself am, I cannot respect that same solitude in others, revere their own identity, and recognize them for the mystery that they are. The harmonious interaction of any individual, as of any community, demands a strong affirmation of both principles. If one is weak the other will dominate; if both are weak the result will be inaction rather than interaction. Just as in any community there will be both sorts of people, the solitary and the communal, so also each one lives a common life and yet also requires time apart, some form of withdrawal. It is the recognition and affirmation of both which allows me fully to realize the extent to which I am separate and alone, and yet also profoundly connected to others in brotherhood and sisterhood.

☙

The holding together of body, mind and spirit is one of the most basic of the tensions in the Benedictine way of life. The Rule tells us that we are made up of these three elements, that we go to God – and also achieve our own full humanity – through recognizing and respecting the role of each element.

This balanced way of living was something written into the daily and hourly routine (horarium) of the monastery; time for work, for study, and above all time for prayer. It promotes rhythm and balance, a pattern of alternating activity, for which I am deeply grateful because it challenges me to become a full person and a whole person. I must learn to respect the whole of myself. If each of these elements is accepted, honoured and enjoyed, each can become a way of reaching God as well as of becoming the integrated human being God is calling me to be.

※

But then I encounter another contradiction. The Benedictine vow of stability calls me to stand still, to stand firmly planted not on any plot of ground (which is likely to be impossible) but within myself, not running away from who I am. Yet in the vow of *conversatio morum* (which literally translated means "conversion of manners" or "conversion of life") I am presented with the necessity of living open to continual conversion, ready to grow and change and move on. On the one hand I find that I must stay still; on the other, that I need continually to change. As I try actually to live in this way Ifind that here I encounter a fundamental tension that I know I can never expect to escape or evade, but one which answers a deep need in me, so that simultaneously I stand firm and yet also I move on.

In the Prologue St Benedict makes it clear that he has unshaken confidence in my use of my natural gifts and free will to serve God: my particular gifts are the actual medium through which God acts on me. Yet he is telling me that I cannot do anything good unless God first turns to me, calls me, extends his grace to me – reminding me that I am a totally dependent creature, my nature powerless without God's grace. Here again I am clearly presented with a tension that runs throughout my life. I am nothing without God; it is his grace that calls me and upholds me. Yet my human nature is good, and God looks to me for the activity that will make use of my gifts. Again, I believe that if I can enter into this paradox and incorporate both these elements into my life I shall escape that passivity that encourages me to do nothing at all and hand everything over to God, or that terrifying compulsion of over-activity that comes from reliance upon my unaided self.

❦

Now from the interplay of these contrasting elements, and from the determination not to let one dominate, comes a vigorous interaction of all which brings with it energy. And in a world in which we see so frequently on the one hand energy directed in so many different directions that it is totally disseminated into some quite frenetic activity, and on the other hand inaction, sometimes to the point of paralysis, it is good to be confronted by the Rule, and by the energy which diffuses the Rule.

For St Benedict does confront us right at the start with the marvellous, challenging and invigorating Prologue. He addresses us all, and calls out to us all with a sense of urgency. There is urgency in Christ's call to us (the Lord calls out and lifts up his voice again), and the urgency which is expected from us in our response (it is a battle and it is also a race: there is nothing passive here). It is time to rouse ourselves from the point to which we have drifted through the sloth of disobedience. It is high time to get up, high time for us to arise from sleep. We must open our eyes. We have above all to run, a word which he uses time and time again.

Run while you have the light of life.
Run on the path of God's commandment.
We must run and do now what will profit
    us for ever

🕉

We must run on, press forward all the time. And here St Benedict presents us with yet another tension. He tells us time and again that it is today that is essential, that it is today which gives us the opportunity, the time and the place for our enounter with Christ. But he is also pointing us forward to a consummation in the future. So, simultaneously with this insistence that we should live fully now comes this vibrant and restless sense of movement and of growth which points us on all the time to our heavenly home, to the place where we really in the depth of our being most long to be. "Are you hastening toward your heavenly home?" he asks in the final chapter.

I find here a mysterious sense of time. I am told about patience and perseverance, about waiting quietly, about living totally in the moment. Yet I am also told about the need to run. Sometimes I feel as though I am being asked to be one of the disciples, leaving everything and rushing forward to follow Christ. Sometimes I feel as though I am being asked to be Mary at the foot of the Cross, standing and waiting. But again I know that I have to hold both together; I have to run and I have also to wait. I also know St Benedict would tell me that ultimately it is only love that makes sense of time. "As we progress in this way of life and in faith, we shall run on the path of God's commandments, our hearts overflowing with the inexpressible delights of love."

❋

It becomes clear that what St Benedict is asking of me, on the one hand, is to live a life of love and service to others, of hospitality which in its widest sense means reaching out to others because I see Christ in everyone. But on the other hand I am also to pay attention to my own need for solitude; to keep "enclosure", which in its widest sense means place and time for withdrawal; to find above all time for contemplative prayer. For what the Rule discloses is a life in which prayer and the constant awareness of the presence of God are never lived out at the expense of concern for the demands of ordinary daily life, of attention both to things and to people. This requires of me nothing less than holding on to a contemplative centre, a heart of prayer in the midst of my busy daily life.

※

There is one further paradox, the ultimate one, that I am asked to live out: the paschal mystery, Christ's death and resurrection. Dying and rebirth is the most fundamental, the most mysterious paradox of all, so mysterious that I shall never come to any full understanding of it in this life. St Benedict tells me to keep death daily before my eyes. Yet Easter is the pivotal point of the Benedictine life, as it is of any Christian life.

Unless I face the darkness I cannot experience the light.
Unless I face death I cannot know new life.

※

As I attempt to live out all these various contradictions day by day, I find it at once easy and manageable, and totally demanding. Again surely that is as it should be, and actually what I would really wish. For until tension enters my life I feel no need to become more than what I am. Until I am stretched I shall not grow. Often it is very painful; often I would prefer to stay with whatever makes the least demands on me. Yet since I know in my heart of hearts that I grow by opposites, not by simple progression along a single line, I welcome the juxtaposition of two texts right at the start of the Rule; the promise that "the way will be narrow" and the promise that "my burden is light". St Benedict does not attempt to suppress the opposition between them. Instead he shows us how they will be reconciled when he quotes from Psalm 118: "I have run the way of your commandments, for you have enlarged my heart." Here then are two contrary affirmations brought together by this subjective solution, by the inner disposition, which is love.

And here at last I touch on the key to everything else. I can say two things about the Rule of St Benedict.

It is all about love.

It points me to Christ.

Perhaps in the end these two statements are no more than two expressions of the same truth. Ultimately the whole meaning and purpose of the Rule is simply "Prefer nothing to the love of Christ".

꽃

Christ is the cardinal point through which everything in the monastery passes: time and place and things and persons, all ordered by Christ. Everything gains its meaning and its significance in and through Christ.

The Christ-centredness of the Rule and of the life

to which it gives rise is overwhelming. Christ stands at the head of every avenue. The way of St Benedict is pervaded with the idea of sacramental encounter with Christ, in liturgy and office, in material things, in the circumstances of daily life, above all in people.

Christ is the beginning and the end, the ground of my being and the goal of my seeking. With Christ all things become possible; without Christ nothing makes sense.

When St Benedict uses that simple phrase "for the love of Christ" he is saying it all, summing up where the whole Rule is leading us. Everything points to that figure of Christ asking to be received, listened to, loved, followed. In the Rule St Benedict is giving us practical help towards creating space for the presence of Christ in our lives. He offers us the opportunity of finding Christ, of experiencing his love. He is showing us the Easter Christ, present to us now, who knows human strength and weakness, joy and pain, and in that humanity reaches out to our own humanity.

※

This Christ is a man who himself lived with tension and contradiction and inner conflict.

> He is a man surrounded by friends who yet withdraws to be apart in the desert.

> He is a son and yet he separates himself from his family and asks "who is my mother and who are my brothers?"

He stays alone with himself through long nights of prayer but still journeys on on a road that he knows will bring him to suffering and to death.

He is the redeemer who on the Cross holds together the vertical, pointing towards God, and the horizontal, arms stretched out to the world.

In Christ all things will be brought together.

In Christ all things will be well.

Living With Myself

To discover how to be human now
Is the reason we follow the star.

Those words of W. H. Auden in *For the Time Being*
find an echo with most of us. To discover how to be
human now today, tomorrow and for the rest of my
life is the reason I follow St Benedict. For he is a man
who had first learnt to live with himself in those
years which he spent as a hermit in the cave at
Subiaco, before the years in which he lived a community life at Monte Cassino as the founding father
of a family of monks. Thus he already knew from his
own experience that most necessary of all human
experience, that unless and until he could live with
himself he could not live with others, and conversely
that unless he could live with others he could not
live with himself.

St Benedict is the great humanist. He believes in
God, but he also believes in men and women, in you
and me. He knew it was impossible to praise God
without at the same time praising his noble creation,
the men and women made in his own image and
likeness. But he is also a great realist, which is why

41

we find we can believe in him. For he begins where we all are, in our weakness and muddle and laziness and confusion. Sometimes it seems as if he is writing a Rule for a community where things go wrong all the time; where people are late, or they grumble, or they get sick, where they complain, where they often need to be rescued. There is often an almost humorous resignation about what people are like and how they behave. So while he knows about human vulnerability and weakness, he also knows about the potential in each of us. This is precisely the starting point of the Rule, that we grow strong through our weakness. Here is something immensely reassuring and unthreatening. For at the same time he holds on to human perfectability. The good in us has been damaged, bruised, but he is showing us the path to recovery. The abbot, who is the exemplar of Christ's love for each member of the community, works with compassion and healing, carrying each one forward in whatever way may be appropriate. So the end is the same for all of us – that we shall run the way to God, building through his grace on our gifts and potential, being continually shaped into that full person whom we most long to become and whom God is calling us to be.

❧

"Our spirituality was never intended to alienate a person from his humanity but rather to uncover it for him," writes a contemporary American living by the Rule of St Benedict, "so that a monk is to become more of a person during his spiritual journey, not less of one." What he says here is equally true of me as well. But for many of us the difficulty is that we live in a society that encourages us to play roles, and this is a game in which it is all too easy to become trapped. Even though I may really know that I can never become whole until I become free, I often find it difficult to see what is happening and to challenge it. The poet Kathleen Raine expresses it well: "I realized that I was the same person whether scrubbing a floor or writing a poem, that my dignity as a being was in no way dependent upon the role which I had at any moment to assume – for all such roles are merely that, and the person free of them all."

It is often so much easier to live with the image that I have created to please myself, and not least to impress other people. Am I ready to let go of appearances? Am I prepared to take off the mask? For Christ challenges this feigned identity, as does St Benedict. The Gospel confronts me with the whole Christ, and the whole Christ demands the whole woman, the whole man.

> Christ loves the whole woman, the whole man.

> Christ wants the whole woman, the whole man.

> Christ loves and wants the whole of me, not the counterfeit self, not the pretend self, not the half self.

One of the reasons that I have been drawn to the Celtic tradition, and have frequently found that it deepens my appreciation of the Rule of St Benedict, is that in their totally simple and unselfconscious prayers I see a people who find it quite natural to present the whole of themselves and the whole of their lives to God. So at the start of the day they will pray:

> Give us, O God, the needs of the body,
>> Give us, O God, the needs of the soul;
> Give us, O God, the healing balsam of the body,
>> Give us, O God, the healing balsam of the soul.

A morning prayer may take the form of a consecration:

> Consecrate us
> Heart and body
> Thou King of Kings, Thou God of all.
> Amen.

> Each heart and body
> Each day to Thyself,
> Each night accordingly,
> Thou King of Kings, Thou God of all.
> Amen.

The totality of the offering of the whole self to God comes across in this great affirmation:

I am giving Thee worship with my whole life,
  I am giving Thee assent with my whole power,
I am giving Thee praise with my whole tongue,
  I am giving Thee honour with my whole
                                utterance.

I am giving Thee love with my whole devotion,
  I am giving Thee kneeling with my whole desire,
I am giving Thee love with my whole heart,
  I am giving Thee affection with my whole sense,
I am giving Thee my existence with my whole
                    mind,
  I am giving Thee my soul, O God of all gods.

❧

Only when I face the fullness of my self can I rest in myself and present myself whole-heartedly to God. Yet I suspect that there are very few people who can easily accept themselves, even though I also know that this is one of the deepest needs of all. "A life without acceptance is a life in which a most basic human need goes unfulfilled", writes Peter van Breemen. "Acceptance means that though there is need for growth I am not forced. I do not have to be the person I am not. Acceptance liberates everything that is in me. Only when I am loved in that deep sense of complete acceptance can I become myself."

If I am appreciated for what I do, what I achieve, I am not in fact unique since someone else can do the same, and probably do it better than I. When my estimation and value of myself depends on what I can produce with my hands or with my mind, then in Henri Nouwen's words I have allowed myself to become "a victim of the fear tactics of the world". This is the self that so often leads me into activity to prove my value. But if productivity becomes my main way of overcoming self-doubt I lay myself open to rejection and criticism, and so to inner anxiety or depression. I am constantly checking myself and my achievements. So my productivity really only reveals how much I am driven by fear of not being up to standard and by an insatiable desire to justify myself. It is only when I am loved not for I *do* but for who I *am* that I can become myself, unique and irreplaceable.

ℜ

Paul Jones, an American Protestant theologian who went to spend six months in a Trappist monastery in the Rockies, was aware throughout his time there of just how much he was continually learning about himself. He found that he was brought back time and again to human frailty, to his insecurity, his jealousy, his resentments. As he lists his feelings in his diary he writes "For all my supposed progress in the spiritual life I do not know how to handle this, even though as I write it, it seems so petty, so insignificant, indeed childish. I must keep clear in myself the perspective of what I am truly about . . . Everything seems to centre in acceptance, and that is what redemption is about."

It is the humble and honest acceptance of my frailty that frees me from pretence, from the effort to impress, from the attempt to justify, from the determination to achieve. What I need to remind myself of time and again, until I am at last convinced, is that I am loved and accepted by God just as I am. Since I cannot be more demanding than God it surely follows that I must love and accept myself. Only then, loved for what I *am*, can I become myself, the unique and irreplaceable person that I truly am.

❦

There can be no more role-playing for those who attempt to follow the Rule of St Benedict, no more hiding behind a mask. We stand daily before God with empty hands, just like the publican. "*Suspice me*, accept me O Lord as you have promised and I shall live; do not disappoint me in my hope." These are the words the novice says on entering the community. They are words that I come back to, time and again, as a prayer for myself. They mean more now that I have learnt that the Latin word comes from the verb *sub-capere*, to take underneath and so with the idea of supporting, raising, and that in Roman usage it was the word for a father taking up a new-born infant from the ground and thus recognizing it as his own. The implication here then becomes one of acceptance and thus of survival. So when I say *suscipe me* it conveys the full depth and warmth of that word. Accept me, receive me, support me, raise me up – wonderful singing words that say everything that I want to say as a prayer for myself. They are words that I understand at one level today, as I say them now, and as I present myself today before God. But they are also like some Eastern *koan* in which the full mystery of what I am saying will only gradually unfold and grow as my own fortune opens up before me.

For the self that I present full face to God is not anything static. If I ask God to accept me as I am now, in the present, I am also able to receive whatever he has in store for me in the future. If I really hand myself over, making an act of personal surrender, asking God to accept me just as I am now, open, vulnerable, powerless, then I shall also be able to receive whatever he has in store for me in the future.

Accepting myself and refusing to run away from myself is in essence what the vow of stability is all about. The three vows which the novice lays on the altar at the moment of entering the community, while he or she says *Suscipe me*, speak to all of us even if we are not living in community, or under any vows other than those of our baptism. They touch basic roots and needs in our humanity, speaking to the intellect, illuminating the spirit, nourishing the emotions. All three interlock and interact one with another. All three relate to one another so that none can go off at a tangent, but rather allows each to strengthen the other.

The three together bring me back once more to the role of tension, the importance of equilibrium, and of holding things together. They show me once again the vital necessity of the right relationship between the parts.

The vow of stability tells me that I must not run away from myself. It tells me to stand still, to stand firm, not in the sense of standing still in some geographical spot, which of course is simply not possible for most of the time in our highly mobile twentieth-century world, but in the more funda-mental sense of standing still in my own centre, not trying to run away or to escape from myself, the person who I really am. Whenever I encounter that insidious temptation to say "If only", whether of the past or of the future, I must firmly put it away from me, and instead tell myself that God is present in my life here, in this moment in time and in this place, and it is no good searching for some other place and time where I believe I might find him. "You have a home," Henri Nouwen reminds us that Christ is telling us. "I am your home . . . claim me as your home . . . It is right where you are . . . in your innermost being . . . in your heart." The more atten-tive we are to such words the more we realize that we do not have to go far to find what we are seeking. The tragedy is that we try to find that place else-where, that we wander off searching for it, and so we become strangers to ourselves, people who have an address, but are never at home. And, we might add, unless we are at home we shall never be able to receive the figure of Christ who stands outside, knocking, waiting to come in.

꭮

But standing still is only part of the picture. I have also to be ready to journey on. So there is also the vow of *conversatio morum* which Thomas Merton called the most mysterious of all the vows. It means continual conversion of life: it means living open to change; it means being ready to face whatever may be involved in responding to Christ's call to discipleship, saying "Yes" to his words "Follow me". I must be prepared to put the past behind me, ready to move forward into the new, however costly that might be. A total and wholehearted "Yes" will mean that I am being asked to walk forward all the time. "Do you turn to Christ?" – that question asked at baptism is a good question for me to ask myself at the moments of the small decisions that make up my life, those occasions when I am faced with something that I might prefer to neglect, reject, evade. But I also know that unless I have the courage to journey on all the time I shall never grow into the person whom Christ has called me to be. The moment in which I feel that I have arrived, that I have succeeded, that I am now at last complete and can feel satisfied, that is the dangerous moment. It is then that I am tempted to stop, to fossilize, instead of recognizing that this growth towards God must go on until the day of my death.

This can be costly. I think that most of the time I like what I know and what I feel safe with. I am frightened by the unknown and the demands that it will make upon me. Change does not come at the time that I might expect it or welcome it. It sometimes seems as though it is going to mean the breaking down of all that I had so carefully built up. But it is just then that God is telling me something that I need to hear. He is telling me that I had been building myself idols, without noticing it, and that however good they were I was still clinging to them. It might be family life with small children, a well loved house, a familiar job, all very good in themselves. But now I may be being told to let go of them, and so be free for something else, the next step forward. And as I let go of these I find instead that in the last resort there is one reality only, and one dependence only, and that is God himself. The God who walks beside me just as he did on the road to Emmaus with those disciples who failed to recognize him; the God who is holding out his arms to me, ready to hold me up when I might otherwise fall. God is there, in the facts. If change teaches me anything at all it is this – that God is there all the time, the Christ to whom St Benedict is pointing me, who stands with hands held out, and with the marks of the wounds that do not go away. Those scars remain as signs of love; they are promises of freedom and new life. That remains the miracle. If stability tells me of the certainty of God, *conversatio* tells me of the unpredictability of God – and both have a role to play in my journey to him.

❧

But how I really find God in all of this – both in the standing still and in the journeying on – must of course depend on my disposition and on my open-ness and willingness to hear and to see and to be constantly aware of God in my life. And this is where the vow of obedience comes in. Really it is no more than listening to God – and listening is after all the way in which the Rule opens. Listen is the very first word of the Rule: listening in its fullest sense; listening with every fibre of my being; listening in all the ways in which God is trying to reach me. This will not only be in words (though a dialogue with God through the scriptures, through daily reading, and particularly through the psalms, is very central to Benedictine life. But also listening through the people whose lives touch mine; through the things I touch and handle; through moments of grace. Do I really take this as seriously as I should? Do I not in fact so often take for granted God's amazing gener-osity? By the evening do I look back on the day, see how God has been there in all my encounters, in all my daily activity, waiting with hands stretched out towards me? And then, I need to ask myself how truly did I hear and respond? For that is ultimately what obedience is about; that I listen, and I respond, and I act on what I hear.

✠

The inter-relationship of these three vows is dynamic. A vital dialectic holds them together. Their strength for me lies precisely in the way in which each needs the others for true balance.

If I stand still without moving on I am in danger

of becoming static, of failing to grow, possibly even of fossilizing.

If I journey on without remaining still in my innermost being I am in danger of becoming a wanderer, someone who is endlessly searching.

If I do not continually stop and listen to the voice of God I am in danger of listening only to my own self, and so failing to discern what he is asking of me.

These three vows are basic to my humanity, answering a fundamental need. For "Give me a place to stand" is a pre-Socratic cry, a deep need in all of us. But then journeys have always been a part of human need, whether the odyssey, the search for the holy grail, or Jung's psychic reality as journeyings on. And then our need to hear and be heard. Can anything be more fundamental than this, almost the first cry of any child, and one that continues so urgently throughout the rest of life?

※

But these vows also carry an even greater significance. While they help me to be human they also at the same time point me away from myself, away from that subtle temptation of self-fascination and self-discovery. They challenge any spirituality from becoming yet one more expression of the contemporary obsession with the self, with self-awareness, with self-fulfilment. Instead they point me to Christ.

> Christ the Rock on which I build.
> Christ the Way I follow.
> Christ the Word I hear.

If I am to put Christ at the centre, as St Benedict would have me to, that then displaces me from the centre. Perhaps I had not noticed how subtle that temptation was, that insidious danger of putting myself at the centre so that the emphasis was on me – me serving God, me trying to be good, in order to please God, me accepting the cross as something imposed by God on his children which I must expect to bear with patience. In other words, me working hard to please God. In prayer perhaps I am actually focusing on myself most of the time, my wants, my needs, my failures . . . But when I put Christ, and Christ's love, at the centre, then that means that I say "Yes" to recognizing that love and letting myself receive that love, standing under that great outpouring of love as I might stand in the midst of a shower of rain or a burst of sunlight. When this "courtesy of love" becomes the most important thing in my life then at last I am beginning to live the way of St Benedict, which is of course simply the Christian life, that life of love which reflects the interplay between the giver and the recipient of love. That is not possible until I know both the source of that love and its object, until I begin to know Christ, and also begin to know my true self, that person made in his image and likeness whom I most deeply and passionately long to be, and whom St Benedict, in his loving gentleness and strength, in his compassionate and at the same time challenging concern for each of us, will help me to become.

This is the risen Christ of Easter, not some abstract and remote God, but the God who saves us by taking on the human condition, who himself knowing how to be human will lead us on and help us too to become more fully human. Throughout the Rule I am being brought face to face with Christ, the risen Christ in all his power and compassion and healing love – the risen Christ who will lead me along the path to the risen self.

V

Living With Others

It is only as I learn to accept, to love and to forgive myself as I really am – the person without the mask, the person who lets go of appearances – that I can accept, love and forgive others with the same reality. "My struggle has been not to be able to allow myself to be fallible," writes that great English singer Janet Baker as she has come to know herself later on in life. "As you get older I think the ability to forgive yourself for being fallible becomes the more possible. This is I suppose the fact and grace of growing into an adult human being – that you don't expect yourself to be perfect." She has at last begun to rejoice in herself. This, in her case, has meant fully accepting that marvellous voice which God has given her as a source of joy and pleasure and life-enhancement, not only for others but also for herself, "a gift of God to make me a whole and happy human being". Accepting this as a sign of love, she goes on to reflect that "what is so marvellous is the feeling of being wholly loved . . . I'm beginning to realize there is no love in the world that can provide you with the sense of being wholly loved, except the Christ love. There is no other base on which you walk forward into the dark. But it's a relatively new thing to discover this divine love within, love which sees you every moment, every second of the day, and accepts you as you are." And then she concludes, "Because I am beginning to learn to love myself as I am I hope I am beginning to love my neighbour."

The giving and receiving of love is at the heart of God's plan and purpose for each of us. Unless this is the true centre of my being I am not living as wholly or as deeply as I should be. It is a phrase that I say to myself so easily, "You are made for the giving and the receiving of love". It sounds so simple. Yet I also know from experience that I shall probably spend a lifetime trying to discover its full meaning and to live it out. But here again, St Benedict, who knows human nature so well, is able to help me.

If the Rule of St Benedict helps me to live with myself it also helps me to live with others. I find a compelling image of this in the fact that after the novice has sung *Suscipe me* that refrain is taken up by the entire community and sung three times. Then the novice prostrates himself or herself before each sister or brother in turn. After accepting oneself that same acceptance is given and received from others.

❧

Love dictates the Rule of St Benedict. It is the best guide I know to the hard work of living with other people and loving them as they need to be loved. St Benedict never promises that loving will be easy. He is totally realistic about the demands and difficulties of any healing and fulfilling relationships. Above all, he has no illusions about the tensions in the art of loving, no illusions about the tensions at the heart of love itself. What he has to tell us does not come across in terms of some abstract moral law or code. Nor does he heap sentimental or romantic expectations on love. He gives us instead a description of how loving relationships are to be fostered in a group of people living at close quarters. In other words he tackles the question of loving at the point at which most of us experience it, that is to say, in the day to day encounter with those amongst whom we have to live.

❦

We learn what this involves by being presented with a portrait. There are a number of chapters which give a vivid picture of the abbot at work, a man whose way of loving is an exemplar for all of us, for the abbot is the good shepherd who holds the place of Christ to the brothers in the community. And he has to live out and show that love in circumstances which are only too familiar to all of us. He is a man under pressure. He carries the burden of administration and of decision-making, and above all decisions about the care of people. From this base we can see that loving people as they really need to be loved is not easy.

❦

We must love each one as they are and not as they are not. This sounds simple and obvious enough. Yet it is surprisingly easy to deceive ourselves and not to recognize the extent to which each person is a mystery, and that we must respect this. Perhaps we once again need to remind ourselves that God is unknowable and inexhaustible, and that if we are all made in the image of God then we too are also ultimately unknowable as well. We must recognize our own inalienable dignity as a God-given gift and respect it.

We need to accept that we are all different. This, which is the message of those personality tests so popular at the moment, is something we could have found already in the Rule of St Benedict. For respect for each individual underlies the whole approach to living with others. It means seeing each single person as an unique creation of God. It means recognizing the worth of each individual. Far too often in the history of Christianity theologians and teachers have given us another message, have dwelt on the unworthiness of men and women, their proneness to sin, their worthlessness.

Yet there is none of this in Christ's teaching, nor the Rule of St Benedict. For the starting point is the same:

> Men and women seen as potentially of the highest value.
> Men and women seen as inheritors of the kingdom.

It is amazing to think that, as early as the sixth century, here is a man who says that community exists for the individual and not vice versa. In an Italy of warring tribes and of social demarcation, in which the place of any individual was determined at birth, and clearly delineated for life, by external marks, St Benedict makes the radical statement that each and every person matters, whether slave or free, Roman or foreigner, whether they own the land or whether they till the soil. In bold letters he wrote across the pages of history that "Every one is sacred and each person has a right to develop to his full potential".

So the abbot tries to handle each one according to his true self. "Discretion" is a gentle word to describe this art, one which asks an almost inspired ability to understand deeply the level at which each person will respond best. It recognizes that in each person, in any particular situation, there is an appropriate level of challenge and support. So the Rule is always saying that someone is special, and should be given special treatment: with concessions and allowances for those who need them, either because they are old or sick or weak or have shortcomings. One must be humoured, another rebuked. "He must vary with the circumstances, threatening and coaxing by turns, stern as a taskmaster, devoted and tender as only a father can be. With the undisciplined and restless he will use firm argument; with the obedient and docile and patient he will appeal for greater virtue . . . He must know what a difficult and demanding burden he has undertaken; directing souls and serving a variety of temperaments, coaxing, reproving and encouraging them as appropriate." (2.25, 32)

✠

control

Reverence is one of the underlying themes in the Rule. In regard to material things it suggests handling with care, and it is not bad description of handling people as well. In practice this may mean distancing myself, both literally and figuratively. It is only too easy to crush, to impose, to manipulate. It may mean allowing someone to make their own mistakes and being prepared to stand back and wait, however painful and difficult that may in fact be. Yet it may be the necessary price of healing.

For we are shown the costliness of healing love when things have gone wrong and the good shepherd goes in search of the sheep. He begins gently with the oil of encouragement, but he may have to go on to the cauterizing iron, and finally it may be that he has to apply the knife of amputation. It is no good shrinking from this. For there is a very real danger that we may be tempted to protect the other person from themselves, not to face them with any sort of honesty about what they are doing both to themselves and to other people. But St Benedict will not let us do this. He knows how wrong it is to over-protect. He says in chapter 69 how important it is to stand aside, and to let the other be themselves. This is not because we do not care about them. The reverse is true. But we have to find the right, delicate balance of concern which does not stifle, does not over-protect. I like the way in which Henri Nouwen tells us how Jean Vanier, founder of L'Arche communities for the mentally handicapped, describes the sort of place that he tries to provide for them.

When Jean Vanier speaks of that place he often stretches out his arms and cups his hand as if he holds a small, wounded bird. He asks "What will happen if I open my hand fully?" We say: "The bird will try to flutter its wings and it will fall and die." Then he asks again: "But what will happen if I close my hand?" We say: "The bird will be crushed and die." Then he smiles and says: "The right place is like my cupped hand, neither totally open nor totally closed. It is the space where growth can take place."

❦

Perhaps we should remind ourselves of what Jesus did with the people he met, and how he never attempted to control or to dominate, "but through his words and his actions he offered them an opportunity to search for new directions and make new choices". And now look at what we so often do to people: we batter them with our demands and expectations, we try to influence them to behave in a certain way, we subtly manipulate them to do the things that will please us. We are in fact trying to control, to improve, though of course we would maintain that it is only for their own good. We are in fact using them to our own advantage and not to theirs – which means ultimately devaluing them.

❧

When St Benedict decrees that the celebration of lauds and vespers must always end with the reciting of the Lord's prayer for all to hear he is insisting that twice a day the monks make this pledge to one another: forgive us as we forgive. We see here the Lord's prayer put into the context of forgiveness as it is in St Matthew's gospel (Matthew 6:12). Commitment to continual forgiveness becomes a constitutive part of the community life, for St Benedict recognises – something equally true for all of us – that forgiveness is needed at two levels. First, that I am forgiven, which frees me from my guilt; and secondly, that I forgive, which frees me from my anger towards others: a two-fold forgiveness whose power releases me and helps me towards healing.

Healing love asks me to take forgiveness seriously; indeed to give it a central place in my relations with others, for St Benedict, realist that he is, knows that it is only too easy for the "thorns of contention" (such a vivid phrase) to grow up. We all know how easily, and really how inevitably, we all hurt one another, sometimes so deeply that the pain stays with us for years afterwards. We also know that this is dangerous, even disastrous. If we leave these hurts untended they will develop into running sores, perhaps even become black cancerous clouds which attack our inner psyche and destroy our energy. We play the old tapes time and again, and base our lives on a negative. Resentment is a powerful force. Mulling over old grievances can so easily become a preoccupation. But St Benedict is adamant that we must not allow ourselves to do this. He is extremely stern about what he calls "murmuring", which I take to be this interminable inner conversation by which we chew over past resentments. Instead there must be forgiveness. The prodigal son is the heart of the Gospel. We must learn to forgive – and time and time again, for it is not as easy as it should be. Yet it is vitally necessary. If we are concerned with healing and with growth then here is the greatest factor to promote it. Failure to forgive is not only harmful to me. It is also disastrous for those involved with me.

※

"It is only we who brood over our sins. God does not brood over them. He dumps them at the bottom of the sea." When God absolves it is something absolute, it is what the word itself after all implies, a total setting free.

St Benedict knows so much about human nature and human relations by giving this central place to forgiveness. Until we forgive we cannot be free. Until we forgive we are enslaved, in chains to the past, in bondage to hurtful memories. We can only be healed through forgiveness, and we can only gain freedom through forgiveness. This does not simply mean believing that I am forgiven; it means experiencing it, realizing that those words "neither do I condemn

you" are addressed to me. Forgiveness is the greatest
factor for growth for any human being.

Without forgiveness there is no love.
Without love there is no growth.
Without growth there is no continuing life.

When in the gospels Christ heals and forgives he also
sends out.

Go, he says, and use your giftedness.
Go, now you are set free for mission.
Go, and live out fully the life that you have been
given.

❧

For the loving that St Benedict shows us is the
serious and demanding task of constantly reaching
out to renew, rebuild, repair. And the Rule makes
it clear that this is not anything that can be post-
poned until we have a little more time, or energy,
or inclination. All the time we need to renew the
covenant, just as the God of the Old Testament
renewed the covenant with the people of Israel, as
the psalms would daily remind the monks. Sustaining, healing and growth are the three marks of
marriage, Jack Dominian tells us. But that is equally
applicable to other relationships too. Sustaining
really means commitment, staying with it, as in the
vow of stability. Healing asks of us this ability to
forgive. And then there is growth – the readiness to

live open to the new (again a parallel with what the vow of *conversatio* is telling us about our willingness to journey on). We must not let marriage, family life, friendship, indeed any relationship, fossilize at some moment in the past. Our loving must be ready to change, however difficult that might prove.

❦

The abbot, the exemplar of Christ to the community, is quite clear that the demands of loving are both tender and tough, the two are juxtaposed in two consecutive chapters in the Rule. He knows that at some point it may be the kindest thing to put in the knife; he knows that amputation may be a necessary part of healing. He also knows that there will be a moment when it is right to hand over the care of a brother who wants to leave the monastery to others who will handle this better than he can.

For letting go is at the heart of loving.
Loving is about freeing.

There are some lines by C. Day Lewis about the necessary parting of parents and children.

Selfhood begins with a walking away,
And love is proved in the letting go.

But of course this is as true elsewhere. Husband and wife may need to be separate so that they can grow out of a "love" that might have been too much about possessing and being possessed. Where there is clinging, possessiveness, the purity of love is lost. To be too intensely close, too attached, is to make impossible demands on the other – the demand that they are to love one totally in a way that will almost inevitably be impossible and so will lead to negative feelings of jealousy or rejection. This is a form of attachment that might have the appearance or label of love, but it actually enslaves and results in suffering.

❧

Baron von Hügel, who was Evelyn Underhill's spiritual director, once said: "The best thing we can do for those we love is to help them to escape from us." If I have the courage to let go of the person I love I believe that we shall find one another again on a level we could never have imagined. For loving and letting go is at the heart of God's love for the world. We must hold on to this as an expression of love at its fullest and truest. It is here clearly expressed by John Austin Baker:

> The way to find fulfilment of the personality is not to escape from pain by refusing to love (which is suicide) or to love and possess what we love (which is self-centredness) but to love passionately with mind, heart and soul and then to endure the pain of letting go.

He then goes on to say:

Since I know what a hard thing is being asked of me here I am tempted to think that only a hard God could ask it of me. But then I reflect how much it tells me about love. The fact that I am held in such a love and that I am free to accept or reject this pattern means that I am the recipient of that freedom of a God who loves me so much that he can let me go – this very same God who also loved and let go the very image and heart of his own selfhood in Christ – which is an expression of loving to the uttermost and letting go.

❄

The Rule helps me to love without judging, without making demands, without wanting to manipulate. It helps me to find within myself a love which accepts, which forgives, which frees. Such a love is only possible because Christ first loved us. The central message that I learn from St Benedict is that Christ is the model for all our loving. It is in and through him that our loving must take place. Underlying is the reality of Christ's own love for each of us. We love because he first loved us. Our love for one another is a reflection of that first, exceptional, unconditional love.

Living With the World

The book of Genesis is almost casual in its assertion that "God created the heaven and the earth and saw that it was good"[1]. The whole way of life towards which the Rule is pointing is giving us this same message. St Benedict helps me to live in the world with a sense of gratitude and thanksgiving, both for creation itself and for all created things – but in such a way that I establish a right, balanced relationship with them. Again he faces me with a paradox: we enjoy because we do not own; we possess because we renounce possession.

❧

The Rule does not call us to heroic deeds. Instead St Benedict is telling me that my way to God lies in the daily and the ordinary. If I cannot find God here and now, in my home and in my work, in my daily routine, in the things that I handle in the kitchen or in the office, then it is no good looking for him anywhere else. That is why the Rule is so concerned with minute directions about the right ordering of daily life in the monastery, chapters which might at first sight seem tedious, irrelevant, remote. For underlying all these instructions about the porter, the servers in the refectory, the right ordering of the psalms or the right sort of help for daily duties, is this principle. Good order, the right use of space and time, and above all the way in which we handle things, all these are essential to finding and to living out a full and fulfilling relationship with the material world around us. St Benedict is not looking for anything spectacular or unusual. He is asking us to sanctify the present moment, just as he wants his monks to sanctify the present moment, whether in chapel, kitchen, library or garden. The monastic cloister is a linkline symbolizing the fact that no single building which serves the community's life is more important than any other, or should claim superiority over any other. All are to be treated seriously and given due respect. In chapter 52, writing of the oratory, St Benedict says "Let the oratory be what it is called; and let nothing else be done there or kept there" (52.1). In other words, he is saying that its essential nature should be respected, not distorted by using it for anything other than its true purpose. That quality of reverence, here shown to buildings, is also made to include tools and altar vessels, food and drink, daylight and night. All things are seen as sacred and God-given. One small phrase sums it up: "He will regard all the utensils and goods of the monastery as sacred vessels of the altar."

❧

"I will not take you out of the world." There are enormous implications here that I can so easily neglect. Christ was a carpenter for most of his life, and those years were not wasted ones. Then I reflect that for me too it would be really very extraordinary if my own Christian life did not grow out of the most ordinary daily round of family life and earning a living. Christianity does not isolate the sacred from the secular. Not only are material things good in themselves, they are also signs of God's loving attention, and they can, if we let them, open up a way to him. God in fact reaches us where we are, at home, in the prosaic reality of our daily lives. Before we start to lay huge spiritual demands on ourselves and present ourselves with some great hurdle in our spiritual life, perhaps we should try to live out our daily lives "tenderly and competently". Those words of Jean Vanier are simple, undramatic words. It is precisely here that their strength lies. But most of us need help to unearth God in our midst, to practise being aware of his constant presence. This is where the relevance of the Rule becomes clear, for the Benedictine life it shows us is undramatic and unheroic; it simply consists in doing the ordinary things of daily life carefully and lovingly, with the attention and the reverence that can make of them a way of prayer, a way to God.

❧

"He who would love must love in minute particulars." In saying this William Blake reminds me that how I organize the little things in my life will very much affect the great vocation. Meals, sleep, mundane chores, all are important aspects in any Christian life that takes the incarnation seriously. The vision of St Benedict speaks to me because it tells me that all the different things I do are valued. When I handle kitchen implements or gardening tools, this typewriter or any other material object, with loving attention, I then look around me and see how full my life is of gifts to be respected and to be enjoyed.

"The handling of my hand" is a small Celtic phrase which also catches this same sense of handling with care and love and respect. So a woman of the Outer Hebrides turns each activity of the day into a prayer.

Bless, O God, my little cow
Bless, O God, my desire
Bless thou my partnership
And the milking of my hands, O God.

Bless, O God, each teat
Bless, O God, each finger
Bless thou each drop
That goes into my pitcher, O God.

When it is time for her to make the butter she does the same.

Come thou Brigit, handmaid calm,
Hasten the butter on the cream;
See thou the impatient Peter yonder
Waiting the buttered bannock white and
yellow.

Come thou Mary, Mother mild,
   Hasten the butter on the cream
See thou Paul and John and Jesus
   Waiting the gracious butter yonder.

꓆

If I try to follow St Benedict I find that I have to
think about the material things in my life, and that I
am being called to establish a right relationship with
all my possessions. I see myself as steward, holding
these things in trust, enjoying but not owning them.
I find this easier to accept in theory than in practice.
But when I do remind myself that all these good
things belong to God and not to me, I find that my
sense of gratitude for the extraordinary generosity of
God brings with it also a sense of freedom. All things
are on loan, all things come from God, and that
includes my own body as well. I have no rights and
I do not possess. Donald Nicholl writes about this:

Once we realize that we own absolutely nothing
. . . a weight is lifted from us and our hearts
grow lighter . . . at least we have made a true
beginning when we can gaze around at all the
possessions, qualities and capacities that are supposed to be ours and recognize that they do not
really belong to us. In fact a good exercise for us
beginners is to scan slowly over the world we
have built around us and say of every item in it
"Not mine; just on temporary loan'; 'this house
– not mine, just on temporary loan; these books

– not mine, just on temporary loan; these fingers – not mine, just on temporary loan; my mind – not mine, just on temporary loan."

❦

St Benedict's criterion for letting a visiting monk stay at the monastery is that "he is content with the life as he finds it, that he does not make excessive demands but is simply content with what he finds" (61.2). Contentment without excessive demands attracts me, for this is exactly the way in which I would really like to live. It implies that I enjoy things as they are without becoming a slave to them. Since I know that they are only on loan I rejoice in them, but I also feel detachment, delighting in them when I have them but not losing my peace of mind should they be taken away. This is real freedom from the tyranny of assertiveness. It is also freedom from the tyranny of appearing to be successful in a world which measures success by signs of outward possessions and prosperity and profit. For if I am going to try to live in this way I am continuously brought face to face with the fact that everything in my life is gift and I am entirely dependent on God as creator and giver.

❦

Yet even as we say "God created the earth . . . and saw that it was good" we must also admit that that statement is no longer strictly true. For we are now living in a world which lacks a vision of the sacredness of creation, and which has lost its commitment to the dignity of life. We can hardly remain blind and deaf to the urgency of this message as we look around us and see the waste and the pollution, the destruction of the environment, and the exploitation, greed and insensitivity towards the world's resources. "We do not need a super-power to destroy us," as Maria Boulding writes, "we can destroy our civilization unaided by giving these forces free play." But what St Benedict is showing us is how to live simply and with a sense of responsibility. What is true of my possessions is also true of the world around me. The Benedictine approach to the world sees it as a gift of God, a gift to be lovingly nurtured so that it can fulfil its purpose in serving the whole human family. We are entrusted with its care. It is our duty to co-operate with its creator for the common good. We must be careful guardians of its resources, neither grasping nor wasting. "We must always remember that the earth is not so much inherited from our parents as borrowed from our children. We owe a debt to the next generation."

✠

The Benedictine way of relating to the earth has always been one of respect to ensure its continual fruitfulness for human beings: it has always been an ideal of good husbandry and of responsible stewardship of land. Benedictines receive the land and all its produce as gift, and it is from this attitude that their good husbandry results.

> To live we must daily break the body and shed the blood of creation. When we do this knowingly, lovingly, skilfully and reverently, it is a sacrament. When we do it ignorantly, greedily, clumsily and destructively it is a desecration. In such a desecration we condemn ourselves to spiritual moral loneliness and others to want.

❧

So Benedictines can still look at the world that God has created and say "It is good", both the material things of daily living and creation itself. Yet so often I am not really as fully alive as I might be to the amazing fact of creation. I do not stop and pay homage to the extraordinary richness and variety in even one very small patch of grass. I do not stop and watch the never ending change of light and colour in just one single hour. This of course asks me to take time, and that is the one thing I am so often unwilling to do. "I do nothing", wrote John Howard Griffin when he was living in Thomas Merton's hermitage at Gethsemani,

> I take Merton's advice and do nothing, just let all this saturate me, wait for it to tell me what to do. I watch, experience, listen to the things about me.
>   You wait, Tom said. You don't go rushing after what is already there. You wait, give it

time, give it time gradually to reveal itself in you. . . . The solitude unites you with the wind in the trees, the rain, the movement of the birds . . . you witness the creator and attend to him in all his creation.

※

When I read Thomas Merton, and especially when I look at the photographs he took, I find a man who knows that if life is to be a search for God then we must begin by learning to see and respect the visible creation that mirrors the glory and the perfection of the invisible God. His photographs tell me how Merton saw the things, the places, the people in his life. To have taken time to look at them with such loving attention was in itself an act of worship, a homage to that world he so totally enjoyed and loved, that he enjoyed and loved for itself and because it mirrored its creator.

The secret, I realize, is that he lets each person, each object, each place be itself, speak for itself. For him every lived moment became a moment of grace. Everything that he saw was allowed its own autonomy and its own fidelity, from the blue Kentucky hills that he could see from his hermitage and the dramatic landscapes he found in Sri Lanka and Thailand, to an old tree stump, a gate, paint-spattered cans or his typewriter. As I begin to see through his eyes I become aware of something he described in *The Sign of Jonas* as "unspeakable reverence for the holiness of created things". He was always insistent on the need "to see directly what is right in front of us". It seems such a simple thing this, to learn how to see, to see more than the eye sees, to see into the essence of the thing itself.

❧

"It was as beautiful a morning as God ever made", wrote Matthew Kelty, another monk of Thomas Merton's community at Gethsemani, as he sat on a hillside watching a brother slowly going up and down with a tractor seeding corn.

> Above me in the trees seven birds were singing in wild abandon, for sheer joy. Beside me in the fenced-in meadow two brown horses were racing back and forth up to their knees in wet grass, kicking and frolicking. The clouds above were massive white and gold. A light breeze was blowing in from the east, moving the light mist ever so gently, for the cool hollows were shrouded in fog. Who was playing most or best? The horses in the dewy field, the birds in the sycamores, the clouds up in the sky? The brother who had gone forth to sow his seed? Or God in his heaven? It does not matter, for all were playing, each in his own way, and a great joy was shared by earth and heaven ... I was singing with the angels. That was real, singing with Christ in his glory, singing with everyone on earth, with the brother on the tractor, with every person on earth ... I sing with them all in Christ.

"I think it pisses God off if you walk by the colour purple in a field somewhere and don't notice it", writes Alice Walker in her novel *The Color Purple*. "People think pleasing God is all God cares about. But any fool in the world can see [he is] always trying to please us back . . . always making little surprises and springing them on us when us least expect it."

❧

"Be so still inside that you can listen at every moment to what life is offering you", Brother David Steindl-Rast says. But the reality is that often we are so busy, so pre-occupied with our own concerns, so self-centred and obsessed with our own immediate world that we miss all the good things that God has prepared for us, and that lie there ready at hand, waiting for us to see them. And we pass them by, they are lost for ever, these gifts. I sometimes wonder if in the kingdom of heaven there is a great room, rather like a vast lost property office, filled with parcels of every shape and form, unclaimed blessings, that God has given us and we have failed to notice, to receive and make our own.

❧

Mindfulness is what the monastic life teaches us. It is such a very simple thing to walk through life with my hands open, my eyes open, listening, alive in all my five senses to God breaking in again and again on my daily life. If the incarnation means anything at all it means this, that God is reaching me through the material things in the world of his creating. Christianity, after all, is the most materialitic of religions. In the eucharist I am given bread and wine. The whole world is potentially a sacrament. For it is through the material things of his world that God chooses to reveal himself. If this is so then I should handle those things with reverence and respect, with joy, with gratitude. And when I do, I find that I am constantly aware of God the giver, the creator who makes himself accessible through the things of his creating, a God who asks us neither to despise nor neglect the temporal order. In St Benedict I find a man whose refusal to escape into any disembodied spirituality makes his Rule immediately relevant to the way in which I want to live. For he is telling me that ordinariness is the path, he is showing me that God lies close at hand, and that I can be constantly aware of his presence, wherever I am and whatever I am doing.

※

"People of praise" is what Walter Brueggeman tells us that Christian people today are called upon to be. A thankful heart seems such a simple thing, and yet I find that it is something that I so easily forget and have so constantly to renew. I no longer let myself be surprised by the sheer miracle that every dawn the sun rises again. If I thought each morning that, like some prima donna, it was positively its last appearance then I might not so lightly take it for granted. When I have lost the gift of wonder I have ceased to live gratefully, and instead I am at war with myself, torn by greed and assertiveness, envious and discontented, ajar with everything and living an unhealed relationship with the world around me. To live gratefully re-lights my awareness and re-kindles my love, for the capacity for true sight cannot really be exercised apart from the practice of love – the capacity to see with love and delight, with wonder and tenderness, and above all with gratitude.

Together and Apart

The image of the enclosure and hospitality are very powerful images for me. In the first I am set apart, I encounter myself in solitude; in the second I am open to others and to their demands on me. These two things speak to me of the tension, the very necessary tension, between my need to be apart and my need to be together. I am reminded of the words that Henri Nouwen quotes from one of the weekly conferences given by John Eudes Bamberger during the six months that he spent in the abbey at Genesee.

> Without solitude there can be no real people. The more you discover what a person is, and experience what a human relationship requires in order to remain profound, fruitful and a source of growth and development, the more you discover that you are alone, and thus the measure of your solitude is the measure of your capacity for communion.

❊

Here is a tension to be worked out between being apart and being together; my relationship with myself and my relationship with others; appropriate self-love and self-protection and appropriate self-giving.

As the exterior world presses in on me I need time and space for myself, time and space to re-create myself, so that I shall be of more value to myself and others. I find that the Rule of St Benedict not only helps me to recognize this need but it helps me as well to impose some sort of balance, to find some sort of equilibrium.

❧

As so often, his help comes not in any theoretical discussion but by way of thoroughly practical example. We are given a very tender portrait of the cellarer, the bursar of the community, the man with the keys of the cupboard. Holding such a central position in a group of men who own no private property, he exercises immense power for good or ill. Monks come with impossible requests, or they want things that are not available. He deals gently with all these demands, he serves people promptly, not wanting to keep them waiting. In all of this he remains *non turbulentus*, not excitable, a phrase used by Isaiah to describe the Suffering Servant. We see here a man who is wonderfully sensitive to the needs of the people he deals with. But he is also sensitive to his own needs. He is ready to delegate if the community is large, turning to helpers whenever he needs them. He imposes limits, "Necessary items to be requested and given at the proper time" (31.18), so that he will not be endlessly available. He knows that there is a line to be drawn and he knows where to draw it.

We are given the same message when we read about how hospitality is to be practised. The Rule is marvellously detailed in its description of hospitality, laying down great care for the reception of the guest, full of love and warmth. He is to be met with all courtesy of love, every kindness shown to him, his feet to be washed by the entire community. Hospitality is a particular Benedictine virtue, "Let all who come be received as Christ" is perhaps one of the most familiar aphorisms of the Rule. And yet the final paragraph is quite clear:

> No one is to speak or associate with guests unless he is bidden; however, if a brother meets or sees a guest he is to greet him humbly as we have said. He asks for a blessing and continues on his way explaining that he is not allowed to speak with a guest (53.23, 24).

Again, there is a line to be drawn. There is a limit to the amount of giving to another. There can be no doubt at all about the respect for the guest, the welcome given, the love shown. Yet there is also respect for one's self and for one's own way of life. The peace and silence of the monastery must be protected.

※

There is a nice balance here of togetherness and apartness, of intimacy and distance. If the life of the community does not go on, there is nothing to give the passing stranger, nothing for him to share or gain from. Its value for him lies precisely in its inner strength, in its certainty that its own way of life has an integrity that must be maintained. No one can be a good host who is not at home in his own house. Nor can I be a good host until I am rooted in my own centre. Then, and only then, have I something to give to others.

I am brought back once again to seeing how vital it is that I take respect for myself seriously. St Benedict is often more gentle than I tend to be, tender and nurturing, ready with concessions and allowances when they are needed. He also shows a gentleness about time that can be far removed from the often harsh way in which I apportion my time. The framework he imposes on the day grows out of human needs. It is made delightfully clear when we find that the time of the night office is determined "so that the brothers can arise with their food fully digested" and be given "opportunity to care for nature's needs" (8.2, 4). This encourages me to stop and ask myself if I am equally respectful of my own humanity, if I handle my own body and its demands as considerately as this. It is only too easy to become so busy and preoccupied in looking after others that I neglect myself and my own demands. Of course it is good to feed the hungry and to care for the needy. But what if I should discover that the person most in need of food and alms is in fact myself? That I stand in need of my own kindness, and that I am the one who needs to be loved? Without this I am likely to be ajar, and no longer at peace within myself. I have lost my inner harmony. This means that I must pay attention to my own peace of mind, for unless I do I am useless to myself and to others. I simply become so over-involved that I have nothing left to give. True quality of life means being able to live for others with sufficient resilience to avoid being drained by them.

※

Those who live closely together know that too much sharing, too much togetherness is destructive not only of the individual but of the community. After years of living, eating and praying with his brothers a Trappist monk wrote of what he called "choral geography". As I reflect on what he is saying I find that there is here something which speaks to me too in the context of family, office, staff room, parish.

One sort of space a monk must have, and it can be expressed beautifully in the dimensions of a church, a cloister, a refectory, a chapter room . . . We ought not to miss the message of choral geography. Two facing choirs, as in church, in chapter, in refectory . . . We face one another in an open, living dialogue with God and yet we keep our distance. For we all need inner space, privacy. Without that we become impoverished.

Another monk makes an analogy with music:

A great piece of music comes across as wonderfully free. An intense discipline is needed to create related sounds, and also a respect for those absolutely vital silences which create space between phrases and make the whole ensemble a manifestation of liberty ... Those who live closely together know very well that there is a great danger when the community insists on too much sharing. It is destructive not only of the individual but of the community.

What one is looking for is a delicate balance between the public and private, between intimacy and distance.

Any community must be poised between these two poles of solitude and togetherness, for they are essential to each other. David Steindl-Rast puts this bluntly:

Togetherness without solitude is not truly togetherness, but side-by-sideness. To live merely side by side is alienation. We need time and space to be alone, to find ourselves in solitude before we can give ourselves to another in true togetherness. [Then he adds] One needs strong roots in togetherness to be solitary rather than lonely when one is alone ... Solitude is aloneness supported by togetherness.

Rilke's lines which describe love as "two solitudes that protect and border and salute each other" beautifully catches this tension. In *The Prophet* Khalil Gibran says of marriage "Let there be spaces in your togetherness". But this is equally true of any relationship.

Sing and dance together and be joyous
But let each of you be alone.
Even as the strings of a lute are alone
Though they quiver with the same music.

Stand together yet not too near together
For the pillars of the temple stand apart
And the oak tree and the cypress
Grow not in each other's shadow.

Yet how often it is difficult for most of us to give solitude any sort of priority in the kind of life that we live today. How we avoid it; how we are frightened of being alone; how easy it is never to let it happen: there is always something or someone to fill the void, even if it is no more than turning to the radio for company. I guess that it is a question of inner conviction as well as external pressure. The world simply does not understand this need to be alone. As Anne Morrow Lindbergh says,

Anything else will be accepted as a better excuse. If one sets aside the time for a business appointment, a trip to the hairdresser, a social engagement, or a shopping expedition that time is accepted as inviolable. But if one says: I cannot come because that is my hour to be alone, one is considered rude, egoistical or strange.

And yet I also know that time for me to re-create myself is amongst the most urgent of all my needs. Only as I find time to live with myself and to love myself will I be able to live with others and love them as they need to be loved. This is not something which applies only to the hermit or the solitary: it is just as true for me in my own life. I have to become my own best friend, enjoying my own company, rejoicing in the person that I am.

❦

But it is only too easy to talk about solitude as something highly desirable, to be sought after, when in fact for many lonely people (and that will almost certainly include all of us at some point in our lives) that will simply not be true. Then being by oneself is neither beautiful nor idyllic. Solitude and loneliness are very different things. We may find ourselves alone, but not from choice. We may find ourselves alone when we long to be part of a family, isolated when what we most long for is to belong.

We live in a world that is full of lonely people. Loneliness is one of the many new diseases of our century. We are told that if we walk down Fifth Avenue, New York and take a count we will find that eight out of every ten people are crying inside.

But to be able to be alone is a very different thing,

and it is probably something that we all need to learn. Perhaps once again the Rule has something to say to us. For here we see the necessity of standing utterly alone before God, totally open. "It is a gift, a rare gift, to be happy utterly alone," Paul Jones said after several months of his stay at Snowmass, as something of the power of that place began to work in him, and as he observed in the Trappists around him the gift of what he called "the hermit heart". It is essentially being able to live creatively with oneself.

※

For if I am estranged from myself then I am also estranged from others too. If I am out of touch with myself I cannot hope to touch others. It is only as I am connected to my own core that I am connected to others. It is only too easy as I walk along a crowded pavement, rush into a supermarket, watch people crossing the road as I draw up at the lights, to dismiss them, to fail to see them as human beings, or simply to pass some superficial judgement on clothes or appearance, labelling them, putting them into some pigeon-hole.

There is a story about the Russian Orthodox theologian Alexander Schmemann with which I find I can only too easily identify. He and his fiancée were sitting side by side in the Paris Métro when a badly dressed and unattractive old woman got on and sat opposite them. Speaking in Russian they began to discuss her and to laugh about her awful appearance.

As she stood up to get off she stopped in front of them and said in perfect Russian, "But I was not always so old or so ugly". Schmemann was shocked, shamed into seeing her as the human person that she actually was and that his callous and judgemental dismissal of her denied.

"Everyone is a reflection of how he or she is seen by others." "The very way you look at people can help to transform them." When Jean Vanier says this he speaks out of his own experience of accepting those whom others might so easily dismiss; of bringing a sense of dignity and worth to those who might otherwise have lived out their lives believing that they were rejected by society.

It may well be that if we are living in a vast city, in a densely populated suburb, on a huge impersonal college campus, we shall be continually seeing people whom we shall never see again, with whom we scarcely pass the time of day, or whom we greet and then pass on. Perhaps for many of us this fleeting, transient, mobile contact is a form of modern community, as transient and mobile as secular society itself. So here is another way of being apart and together, something at which we have to work because it is there, a reality of present-day existence. But it is only as I am warm and comfortable in myself, only as I am happy with myself and at home in myself, that I can look on these strangers with warmth and love, see Christ in them, and acclaim them in this passing moment as sisters and brothers in Christ.

Gift and Grace

In the Prologue to the Rule St Benedict writes with great energy, excitement, urgency. It feels as if he is almost breathless in his concern to catch our attention, and as his ideas come tumbling out they seem to jostle one another, contradict one another. He seems on the one hand to be quite clear in asking whether we "are ready to give up our will, once and for all", and he tells us that those who fear the Lord "do not become elated over their good deeds; they judge it is the Lord's power, not their own, that brings about the good in them. They praise the Lord working in them, and say 'Not to us, Lord, not to us, give the glory, but to your name alone'". Yet on the other hand he speaks of "the good gifts which are in us" and tells us that if we wish to reach the kingdom "we will never arrive there unless we run there by doing good deeds". So I am also being confronted by my worth, and the worth of God's creation of which I form a part. On the one hand I am being reminded of my good gifts, my good deeds, and in the same breath I am being reminded of my dependency.

[handwritten margin note: Roman Catholic persp.]

☧

"First of all, every time you begin a good work, you must pray to him most earnestly to bring it to perfection." St Benedict is asking me to admit that I cannot do anything on my own. I am to turn to God, to seek his aid, to throw myself on his mercy and to rely on his grace. Such an admission of dependency is not one that I find immediately attractive, or one that comes naturally, particularly today in a society which prizes a tough and self-reliant individualism. What is being asked of me here, right at the outset of the Rule, is something which St Benedict is going to elaborate in much greater depth in chapter 7, that chapter on humility which gives us the key concept, the lynch pin, around which the life of each monk and of the entire community turns.

Humility at first sight seems a threatening word. It is certainly not a word with which we are immediately comfortable. It seems to imply the giving up of my own will and my personhood, with its claims of full autonomy. It is asking for self-surrender, a word that has unfortunate overtones in the English language, for it always seems to carry a suggestion of defeat, of submission. But the French equivalent, as one recent writer reminds us, gives a quite different sense. *Se livrer* is much more positive. It means to hand over or to deliver oneself over to, with the connotation of a freely chosen act of love. Thus to surrender is essentially a total turning to God in self-giving, a response to a gesture of love.

❧

And yet, like Atlas trying to carry the whole world, I have been mistakenly trying to earn that love, and putting upon myself the vast burden of making myself worthy to be loved. Peter van Breemen, in making this analogy, says, "I would like to say to Atlas, 'Put down that globe and dance on it. Lay down your load . . .' We do not have to earn God's love; neither do we have to support it". We have simply to receive it.

This is the mystery of the Christian life, to receive a new self, which depends not on what we can achieve but on what we are willing to receive. Here is another paradox. I gain my true identity by losing myself for Christ's sake. I let go of the false self, with its claims for full autonomy, and instead I find my true self. Here is God's reversing action once again.

> The empty are filled.

> The poor are made rich.

> To ascend means to descend.

❧

"The false self is the prison from which one must escape in order to reach the true self, and God. For if I find him, I will find myself, and if I find myself, I will find him." Thomas Merton here faces me with one of his favourite themes, one that he so frequently wrote about because he knew how central it must be to anyone exploring the way to God. It brings us back again to the Genesis myth, to the

Garden of Eden, and to the serpent's seduction, "You will be like gods" (Genesis 3.5). It is this illusion of omnipotence which alienates us from God and from our true selves. The journey by which we discover God is also the journey by which we discover, or uncover, our true self hidden in God. It is a journey that we all have to make.

It is so easy to play the world's game which is the power game, the game which depends on setting myself apart from others, distinguishing myself, seeking the limelight and looking for applause. I find that it is only too easy to become compulsive in my continual need for affirmation, for more and more affirmation, as I anxiously ask Who am I? Am I the person who is liked, admired, praised, seen as successful? My whole attitude towards myself becomes determined by the way in which others see me. I compare myself with others, and I try to emphasize what is different and distinctive about me. Those three temptations which Christ faced in the wilderness are equally my own temptations:

> to be relevant
>
> to be spectacular
>
> to be powerful.

Am I able, like Christ, to put them down?

Am I prepared to shed all these outer shells, of false ambition, of pride?

Am I ready to admit that the mask is a disguise put on to cover up the insecure self? and the armour a shield to protect the vulnerable self?

Am I ready to receive a new self, based not on

what I can achieve, but on what I am willing to receive?

※

Humility is facing the truth. It is useful to remind myself that the word itself comes from *humus*, earth, and in the end simply means that I allow myself to be earthed in the truth that lets God be God, and myself his creature. If I hold on to this it helps prevent me from putting myself at the centre, and instead allows me to put God and other people at the centre. For if I want to return to God I must reverse the destructive journey of Adam and Eve which began with that subtle temptation to be as gods. It is this which has brought about the divided self, the self in disobedience to God. If I am to reject this it will mean embarking on a ruthless campaign against all forms of illusion, all forms of self-deception, and this could be a terrifying undertaking. Indeed, unless I am prepared to undertake this with total dedication it is hardly worth beginning, for it will involve my "re-birth in integrity", and that will take a long, long time. Moreover, if in setting out on this path I am doing nothing more than imposing upon myself yet one more challenge this will become self-defeating. If I am continually checking on how well I am progressing then I have merely set myself one more ambitious goal, and exchanged one tyranny for another. I have succumbed to the "journey to perfection" message, and in the end this may be little more than self-fascination under a new guise.

❦

"This process of deliverance."
"A radical demand for disengagement."

These phrases carry the connotation of freedom: of being delivered from the trap, the snare, the net – all those images which the psalms use to such effect. St Benedict wants to release me from the clutches of self-fulfilment and self-assertiveness, so that I am set free, free to love. But this exodus towards freedom is painful, and it is painful because all the time I am being stripped. Every angle of my self-sufficiency has been stripped away. Every element of my self-reliance has been taken apart quite ruthlessly. It has meant death to self-dependence, and in its place dependence on God.

At each step of the way I discover that what matters is not what I can achieve but what I am willing to receive.

At each step of the way I discover that this is the work of God, continually forming and re-forming, shaping and re-shaping.

❦

It is a never ending process this, and there is never one moment when I can congratulate myself and say that now at last it is finished, that I have arrived.

An English Benedictine today tells us that he was to find that the really difficult part of entering the novitiate – and throughout his monastic life since – was not the outward or bodily austerities, as he had feared, but something much more demanding, the stripping of self, the grappling with the "old man", the resistance within and the struggle as the Lord shaped the old into the new. "The long process of discovery, and of being discovered by God, was truly beginning in a fumbling but real way."

The life towards which St Benedict points us will be a series of doors opening all the time, and very often they will look like contradictory doors, for the Rule never promises that we shall escape the contradictions. How do I maintain myself as a person of energy and activity, and also give myself up and hand myself over? How do I give up power and yet remain power-filled?

God is asking of me good deeds, and he is also asking total dependence. "Whatever good work you begin to do beg of him (Christ) with most earnest prayer to perfect it." At the end of chapter 4, in which St Benedict has given the tools that we shall need as workmen, he concludes, "Never to despair of God's mercy" (4.73). So constantly throughout the day I turn to God, "O God, come to my aid". I am living vigorously, with the whole of myself, with all my human nature, my gifts and my potential. Yet I am also aware of my dependence on God, my reliance on his mercy, my need of his grace.

As I hold these two together I find that from the interplay of my own nature and God's grace comes

the energy that helps me run the way to the Kingdom. Rejoicing in the human person who I am, and
aware of God's grace available to me moment by
moment, whatever I do and wherever I am, my
prayer is one of total and utter reliance on God – "O
God come to my aid". But not said passively, rather
triumphantly. "O God, perfect in me the work that
you have begun."

Desert and Marketplace

I find the images of the desert and the marketplace speak to me very powerfully of my need for withdrawal, for times of solitude and silence and contemplative prayer, while at the same time I am engaged in all the noise and pressures of ordinary daily living. If I am to survive all the demands that a busy, active life makes upon me, then I must make sure that I also take seriously the demands which a contemplative life of prayer makes. The two must somehow be held together. Prayer is the anchor which brings the inner strength to my daily activity; my daily activity informs that prayer and anchors it in the reality of today's world.

OK. Now pray. This is the whole doctrine in the Rule of St Benedict. It's all summed up in one phrase: "If a man wants to pray, let him go and pray." That is all St Benedict feels it is necessary to say about the subject. If you want to pray, pray.

Here Thomas Merton is telling us much about his own way of praying, a man of prayer who was also so totally involved in the contemporary world. It is good to remind ourselves that St Benedict plunges into the subject of prayer in chapter 8 of the Rule, with no sort of introduction or preliminary exploration of the subject. Yet in placing it where he does he is in fact making a most important statement about how we should approach the whole question of prayer. For it follows on immediately after chapter 7, on humility, that chapter which has taken us on a relentless climb (which is also at the same time a descent), which leads us along the path of self-knowledge and forces us to face the truth about ourselves. At the end of it all we stand before God, in his truth and in our own truth, waiting like the publican with open hands. In the juxtaposition of these two chapters St Benedict is actually telling us a great deal about the starting point of prayer. He has asked us step by step to open all our inner doors, to surrender all self will, to make space for God. This is precisely what he himself had first learnt. We are given just a glimpse of this when in the Dialogues (the nearest thing we have to any sort of biography) St Gregory tells us that St Benedict lived with himself, in constant watch over himself, always maintaining himself in the presence of his creator. This is what he would wish for all of us too. He wants to lead us into our own centre, to hold us there in the constant presence of God, hearing him and responding to his voice. Come, says Psalm 95, sung each morning in the monastery,

Come today if you would hear his voice, harden not your hearts. Once again St Benedict is reminding us of the centrality of the Word, of our need to listen, to hear, to respond.

> This is a life of continuous dialogue with God.
>
> This is a life of total openness to God.
>
> This means walking with God at every moment of the day.

✠

This ideal and promise that St Benedict holds out to us, that we should grow into men and women of prayer, makes prayer both the foundation and the goal, the root and also the fruit, of all we do. This is the *opus Dei*, the work of God, taken in its fullest sense to mean not simply the liturgy but the whole of life and work as God's own. It is a way of living that will never be possible until we know how to be still and silent. "It becomes the disciple to be silent and to listen" (6.6). This is the interior quality of tranquillity which is caught in that lovely small phrase *in simplicitate cordis*, in simplicity of heart. I think it means that more and more whatever is inessential falls away, and instead prayer becomes increasingly simple and uncomplicated self-surrender – surrender to love. This is where St Benedict is leading us. He has promised in the Prologue that we should be led on towards "unspeakable sweetness of love", and what follows in the main body of the Rule presents us with a practical guide to living out a life of love.

❦

Prayer and life cannot be separated one from the other; both are rooted and grounded in love. The love which we find in the Rule is never an abstraction. It is lived-out love, lived out in the context of our daily life and work, above all our daily contact with other people. The daily work described in the Rule is not simply that of toiling in the fields, which has come rather romantically to be associated with the monastic life. St Benedict would actually rather leave such matters as the gathering in of the harvest to hired labourers. The work of the monastery in fact includes a varied range of occupations and makes use of a wide spectrum of skills. There are young children to be taught. There is the scriptorium to be kept up. There is a heavy burden of upkeep and administration. He sets principles for the pricing of the goods made by the craftsmen in the monastery. There is work in the infirmary and the guesthouse. Much of the work that he describes in fact is looking after other people, welcoming visitors and travellers, feeding the hungry, nursing the sick – who may be querulous and difficult. There is nothing sentimental in his attitude to what may be involved here. He is in fact describing life as most of us experience it: a ceaseless round of daily duties, cooking and then serving and then washing up; constant attention to the needs and claims of others, and all this probably in addition to the particular job for which we have been professionally trained.

St Benedict is asking us to pray through all of this. Prayer undergirds and supports this life of activity. "Whenever you begin to do anything say a prayer" (Prol. 4). Meals begin and end with prayer. Routine duties are prefaced with prayer; the porter greets the guest or the visitor at the gate with a blessing. Material things are handled with as much love and reverence as if they were sacred vessels of the altar. All these short moments of prayer are moments of re-focusing. They are moments to recall God's presence. St Benedict's way to God does not live in any particular mystical experience, but in all the ordinariness of daily living. Prayer is a dimension of a life lived progressively for God.

❦

"The more we receive in prayer the more we can give in the active life." These words come from Mother Teresa, a woman whose own life has been exposed to immense and incessant demands. She would tell us that there is nothing mutually exclusive about giving a priority to contemplative prayer and being totally involved in the world. The two are in fact complementary; the one supports and makes possible the other. The interaction of contemplation and of activity are two sides of the same reality. Brother David Steindl-Rast would tell us that the contemplative vision without practical realization is barren, and service without clear vision is mere meddling. Cardinal Basil Hume would tell us that the monk is safe in the marketplace because he is at home in the desert; he is valuable in the marketplace if he preserves a nostalgia for the desert. To the degree that he learns from the desert he will have something to sell in the marketplace.

❧

When Thomas Merton writes of "the spring and the stream" he uses an effective image to illustrate this. Unless the waters of the spring are living and flow outward, the spring becomes only a stagnant pool. If the stream loses contact with the spring which is its course, it dries up. Contemplation is the spring of living water; action is the stream that flows out from it to others. But the water is of course the same in both. This is equally true for us. If action is out of touch with an interior source in prayer it eventually becomes arid and barren, and we find ourselves the victims of busyness, frenetic over-activity. But conversely, if our prayer becomes cut off from action it is cut off from life. Here is the equilibrium of contemplation and action.

❧

"To see with the heart of Christ is perhaps the best definition of contemplative vision." This continuous encounter with Christ, this dialogue of continually listening in whatever way his voice may reach us, will help us to learn to see the face of Christ in all whom I meet,

learn to find Christ in the things I handle,

learn to touch and taste and feel Christ in my daily life, even in the most improbable encounters and in the most unlikely situations.

learn to see the world with the eyes of Christ and to love the world with the heart of Christ.

✠

Only the contemplative vision growing out of times of solitude and silence makes possible a life of activity in the world. We are confronted once again with a paradox, one which is fundamental to the Benedictine way of life. But the Rule helps us to hold the two together. It shows us action springing from stillness, activity growing from the prayer of the heart. It is not always an easy tension. It is not always easy to hold on to that equilibrium and to keep the balance between the two.

✠

Yet this equilibrium is a very necessary witness in a society which expects to solve its problems by technology and activism, a society which neglects the inner in favour of the cosmetic, and which values the functional and the streamlined far more than the spiritual. Perhaps one of its most important outcomes is that it helps us to beware of hasty solutions. It encourages us to watch and wait, ponder and reflect trying to be aware of what is going on, and of God's place within it, before rushing into "doing something about it". Action without this awareness is more likely to grow out of confusion or fear or self-interest; it is less likely to be grounded in God.

❦

When he was abbot primate of the Benedictine Order, Archbishop Rembert Weakland said that he found the oasis theory – the Benedictine community as a place to get away from the world in order to be with God – giving place to the focus theory – that is to say, seeing the world's problems in a deeper light, above all listening to God in prayer before immersing ourselves in the world's problems.

> The true contemplative is not less interested than others in normal life, not less concerned with what goes on in the world, but more interested, more concerned. The fact that he is a contemplative makes him capable of a greater interest and a deeper concern ... He is not easily involved in the superficial confusion which most men take for reality.

This was something which Thomas Merton knew about, and of which he wrote from his hermitage in the woods outside the monastery at Gethsemani. He then goes on to make this important clarification,

> This does not mean that the contemplative mind has a deeper practical insight into political or

economic affairs. Nor that the contemplative can beat the mathematician or engineer at their own games. In all that seems most practical and urgent to other men the contemplative may distinguish himself perhaps only by ineptitude and near-folly. But he still has the inestimable gift of appreciating, at their true worth, values that are permanent, authentically human, truly spiritual and even divine.

He concludes that what this means is that the contemplative does not set himself or herself up to be a specialist but rather to be a complete and whole person, with an instinctive and generous need to further that same wholeness in others, and in all mankind.

꧁

St Benedict tried to discern the needs of his time and respond to them. His reaction was not a negative one, even though he was writing in a period of decadence and disintegration. His concern was less to pronounce on the world situation than to show concretely the correct stance towards it – an attitude of "interior openness to the world".

꧁

The Rule of St Benedict will never lead us into setting up an alternative society, however attractive that might sometimes seem to be. Far from it. We are being asked to do something which is in many ways much more difficult. We are being asked to walk free of the structures and aspirations of contemporary society while still living in the midst of it. We are being asked to become transforming agents within human society rather than revolutionary ones acting outside it. We are not being invited to become marginal people. We are right here, at the centre of our world, and being at the centre means standing at the point of equilibrium, holding the balance between two forces.

St Benedict never neglects action in favour of contemplation, any more than he neglects the hermit spirit in favour of community life, or indeed any of those dualities which have formed the theme of these meditations. Sometimes I feel that what St Benedict is showing us is like some great wheel in perpetual motion. Solitude becomes communion, communion becomes solitude; silence leads to dialogue, dialogue leads to silence; prayer leads to commitment to the world, commitment to the world leads back to silence. So the movement of continual interaction between the inner and the outer life is maintained in one continuously flowing movement.

Here is a model of integrated Christian living.
Here is a model of life lived out according to
  Gospel values.
Here is a holding together of the polarities which
  is of course nothing less than the living out of
  the biblical paradox on which the Rule is based.

St Benedict is giving me a yardstick, gentle yet forceful and always thoroughly critical, with which to confront the questions of power and property, political problems and personal relationships. He challenges me to measure myself against the fragmenting and destructive tendencies which I see going on in the world around me. He never promises easy answers, he never promises escape from the contradictions. Perhaps this is not a message of Christian comfort but of Christian discomfort.

I live in a complex, consumer society, which exploits both people and the earth itself. St Benedict would tell me that I can live simply and with respect and reverence, for people, for material things, for the environment. I can live with concern, responsibility, stewardship.

I live in a highly competitive and individualistic society, and one that is constantly mobile and changing. I can refuse to live under pressure like that. I can try to be stable, not only in my innermost self, but in my relations to those around me, and in my continuous search for God.

I live in a world of injustice and exploitation, where people are denied the right to live with honour and dignity, a world divided by race, colour, class. I can refuse to live by divisions like this, for I try to find the face of Christ in all I see.

I live in a world in which the churches are split and torn apart. The Rule of St Benedict comes from the undivided Church of the past, and it points me on to the undivided Church of the future, and I must try to play my part in helping that search for unity to grow in my own lifetime, while still remaining faithful to my own tradition.

I live in a world of battering noise, insistent media claims for attention, and endless words of confrontation, constant talk and ceaseless chatter. I can try instead to become a listening person, listening to those around me, and listening above all to God.

I live in a world that is angry, fear-ridden, distracted. I can try instead to carry a heart of stillness, an awareness of God's presence and his gaze upon me. So that I hold on to the contemplative vision even in the midst of the most busy and active daily life.

X

Death and Life

Behind the altar on the east wall of the chapel of a Trappist monastery high up in the Rocky Mountains, on the right hand side of a stained glass window of Our Lady, there hangs a simple wooden cross. It will stay there until it is taken down to mark the grave of whichever brother is the next to die. Until then it hangs on that wall so that whenever the monks turn and face the altar they also turn and face this very simple and immediate symbol of their own death.

✠

Present therefore in their daily celebration of the eucharist and at the saying of their offices is this reminder that death is part of life. It is of course a vivid visual statement of what St Benedict is saying in the Rule, "Keep death daily before your eyes" (4.47). But he is also simultaneously saying, "Look forward to holy Easter with joy and spiritual longing" (49.7). So once again he expects us to hold two things in tension. Death and life are inseparable. Dying and behold we live. Here is the ultimate in contradiction. Here is utter foolishness to the point of absurdity. We lose our life to gain it.

But how right St Benedict is in insisting that we remind ourselves of this every day. For this paradox, this ultimate in contradiction, is not limited to the one event of Christ's own death and resurrection. Nor is it true of us only when, at the end of our lives, we die in the hope of resurrection and of new life. It is also true throughout our human lives.

> If I want to find my life I must be ready to lose it.
>
> Dying makes new life possible.
>
> So, let go, do the necessary dying, and a fuller, richer life will be given. /

※

This is really such an extraordinary claim that I am often tempted to ask whether it really can be true that death brings life, and that dying leads on to new life. It is something that I have heard so many times. But it still remains such an amazing paradox.

> That life can be found *in* death.
>
> That it is the actual process of dying that brings new life.

But then I reflect that if I am ready to follow Christ it means that in any case I do already live in a way that the world would call foolishness, a way in which the world's generally accepted values are reversed and turned on their head.

If we are to be caught up in the paschal mystery day by day, which is what I know St Benedict would wish for all of us, then we must see it in the context of patience and of suffering. Those wonderful words with which the Prologue ends set this out:

> Never swerving from his instructions then, but faithfully observing his teaching in the monastery until death, we shall through patience share in the sufferings of Christ that we may deserve to share in his kingdom.

I am grateful for this. It brings together two realities: that the world in which I live is a world of sin and suffering; that the God I follow is the God of love. If I am trying to follow the way of St Benedict then I too find myself caught up at the heart of this mystery.

※

None of us can escape suffering. That is certain.

> In a certain village a young boy fell ill and died. His mother was inconsolable. Many of her friends tried to comfort her, but she said nothing would ease her grief unless her son was brought back to life. She went to the doctor, but he shook his head and said it was impossible. The wise woman with her herbs and spells said it was beyond her power, and so did everyone else the mother approached. Eventually she came to the hut of an old monk living as a hermit deep

in the forest and asked him if he could restore her son to life. "Certainly," said the monk. "What do I have to do?" the woman cried, delighted that at last someone was able to help her. "Go back to your village," the monk said, "and bring me a cup of milk from a house which has never known suffering, and I will restore your son to life." The woman set off thinking of all her happy neighbours. But as she went from hut to hut even the liveliest of families had to tell her that pain, suffering and death had at some time visited them, and though they were joyful now, it had not always been so. The woman went back to the monk with an empty cup. "Could you not find one house without suffering to give you a cup of milk?" he asked. "No," she answered. "Now I see that there is no life without suffering, and no suffering that cannot be overcome."

The promise of the Kingdom is not that we shall escape the hard things but that we shall be given grace to face them, to enter into them, and to come through them. The promise is not that we shall not be afraid. It is that we need not fear fear.

❦

The cross is failure at its starkest. Christ hangs there with a couple of other failures on either side. To all human appearances this is the final failure. Death on a cross – for Greeks and Romans the lowest, the most despicable form of execution. If I put aside the memory of those great Renaissance canvases; if I forget the little silver crosses that so many people today choose to wear round their necks for decoration, or worse still, use as ornament for earrings; if I forget the sentimental representations of Jesus on the Cross which coloured my childhood imagination of the scene; if instead I place myself at the foot of the Cross, and try to recapture something of its original horror, then what do I see? A man hoisted between earth and heaven; the terrible stretching which pulls him in two directions; the strain on the muscles; the pull on the hands; the nails driven into the wrists ... A man hangs there in weakness, excruciating pain and suffering, total vulnerability, final failure. Where is the triumph, the power, the world acclaim we might expect in a king?

Yet vulnerability and failure are precisely the materials with which God can work. St Paul is constantly aware of his own weakness and poverty, indeed sometimes he seems almost to flaunt it, seeing it as the base from which he can proclaim the riches of God. "But we have this treasure in earthen vessels, to show that the transcendent power belongs to God and not to us" (2 Corinthians 4:7). "We are afflicted in every way but not crushed; perplexed but not driven to despair; struck down but not destroyed." (2 Corinthians 4:7–9). So not merely are the weaknesses of the body no handicap, they actually become the hallmark of St Paul's authenticity as Christ's apostle, "because by uniting him with Christ's weakness and death it enables both the death and the power of Christ's resurrection to be continually present". /

❧

As I try to accept my own vulnerability the surprising thing is to discover that I am not unique, and that others who outwardly seem so successful, so composed, so altogether at one with themselves, in fact on closer acquaintance are just as vulnerable as I. John Howard Griffin, at work on Thomas Merton's papers in the hermitage at Gethsemani, wrote "The world demands in each an illusion of strength that amounts to an illusion of invulnerability . . . But the reality that I face here is the reality of my vulnerability."

Now while in my experience vulnerability is good, this is not necessarily true of suffering. What I find difficult – not simply unhelpful but positively undermining – is to be told (particularly at those times when I am in the depths of despair) that suffering is somehow good in itself, that it is ennobling or purifying or to be welcomed because the bottom of the pit is a very good place to be. Sometimes this seems to be said in tones of complacency, sometimes given rather romantic connotations. But in either case I do not find it helps. I think it is much better to be honest, to admit that suffering can so often be destructive, diminishing, demoralizing, to be prepared to say that it does not automatically transform. In fact the chances are that at the time when I was going through a period of suffering like this it is extremely likely that I shall become insensitive, self-absorbed, inconsiderate of others, difficult to live with.

✠

There are times when, whatever I try to do about it and however much I try to resist, whether by trying to lay it down or else by trying to live with it creatively, the only reality seems to be darkness, emptiness, depression, panic. These times are hard. There is nothing romantic about sleepless nights and colourless days. And God is, or seems to be, absent. As I struggle with this I find that what I most long to do is to shake my fist and shout "Why me? Why should life be so unfair?"

✠

Then in quieter moments I ask myself why I should expect to be given special treatment, why I should ask for immunity. Christ was hurt. Christ suffered – he suffered wrongfully. If I have said Yes to his call to discipleship I should remind myself of the cost of that discipleship.

At times like this there is nothing to do except wait, and wait patiently, reminding myself that the word for patience comes from the Latin *patientia*, suffering. This is the time of Holy Saturday, which I tend to forget about because it receives strangely little attention. But between Good Friday and the dawn of Easter morning there is this long, long time of waiting, when it seems that nothing happens.

❦

The suffering of which the Rule speaks is this waiting, this *patientia*, it is a sharing in the suffering of the Cross, a suffering which leads to transformation because it is tender and open. This has nothing in common with a suffering which is neurotic and self-perpetuating, which feeds on self-pity, which fails to let go of past hurts and wrongs, but clings to them almost as if they were nourishing, but nourishing of course in a way that is destructive. This is suffering and pain to no purpose whatsoever. This is nothing more than self-inflicted death which can never lead to resurrection. This never looks beyond itself, and so it cannot open up to the healing power of the Cross. There is one thing that I must never forget, and that is that Christ himself never embraced the Cross as an end in itself; only as the means to an end.

❦

Stability now has a vital role to play; in fact it now becomes the more urgent. It is no good throwing myself into frenetic activity, no good rushing from one thing to the next, or running from one place to another, hoping desperately that *there* or *then* it will all begin to look rather different. I carry my own inner landscape with me wherever I go. The next town, or country, or even continent, makes no difference. Instead I must stay still, and wait in hope that in its own time

> the yeast will work,
> the seed will germinate,
> the new will emerge from the old.
> For the miracle is that it does happen.
> The mystery is that new life does follow death.

This is a mystery which most of us discover not once but many times over, we live through not once but time and time again throughout our lives. There are some things that we can never escape. T. S. Eliot called them the lesser deaths. Teilhard de Chardin spoke of diminishments. We all of us know them. They take different forms, these small deaths that are the precursors of our final death. They are generally undramatic and unheroic. They are often quiet, painful, threatening. They are nearly always associated with loss.

❧

> Christ wept twice – over Lazarus, over Jerusalem.
> He wept over loss, and over the prospect of loss.

It is good to be reminded that we all go through this experience of loss in our life not once but many times – and each time it feels a little different. There is no defence against loss or bereavement each time when it actually happens again. "Being human is essentially living in an *exodus* situation."

"Leaving is a part of life," Peter van Breemen writes. "We have to ready ourselves in many minor rehearsals for the final farewell which is the only absolute certainty of everybody's life ... Look at Abraham. God says to him, 'Leave your country, your family and your father's house for the land I will show you.'"

The leaving is hard. We all know this. We are happy where we are. Things are going well, we are being used, we feel loved and secure. And then God says, "Leave it all. Leave and go forward into your unknown future." This may well be the start of a time of wandering, of uncertainty, of feeling that the familiar landmarks have gone and the new ones are not yet in place. Then it is good to turn to others and to see how they felt in a similar situation. It is the conviction of the writer of the book of Exodus – and of many other writers since – that in fact God was there all the time, in the wanderings, in the darkness, in the desert, in the fear at the new and strange, when a certain nostalgia for an earlier life with all its certainties – for after all, with the Israelites slavery did have its own inbuilt certainties – keeps alive the memories of the past. But in the end of course the exodus brought the Israelites to the promised land, just as in the end we are also brought to a place of new perspective, new growth, new opportunities which we would never have imagined possible while we were still caught up in the journey itself.

🝞

Death and life are part of the natural order of things, both in human life and in nature. The human body reconstitutes itself afresh every seven years by the death of every particle and the birth of new cells. The seed is thrown into the cold ground so that the shoot can grow. The fruit tree is cut back so that its fruit can yield more abundantly. Christian baptism, with its symbolism of entering into the waters of death, speaks of dying to the old so that the new life is made possible. It does us no harm to think for a moment of what human birth involves. To the baby being born it must feel like some terrible kind of death as it is wrested from the only sort of life that it has known, wrenched from the safety of that enclosed space into the open air, from the security of darkness into blinding light and noise. It cannot possibly know that life in the womb is being exchanged for a life that will be infinitely more rich and free. What feels like the pain of dying may also be the pain of being re-born.

🝞

There are moments in the year, in the natural year and in the liturgical year, when we are made particularly conscious of the dying that is happening all around us and into which we are caught up.

Matthew Kelty tells us that the feast of John the Baptist has always been a particular favourite with the monks because it comes just at the time (it falls on 24th June) when the sun first begins its journey down, a dying which we all know will eventually lead to life.

> The monk sees in the plunge into night his own way into the darkness of God. The inward journey has all the dressings of death, a decrease which, like death, hides the truth of growth into life.

So at the turn of the year as the nights get longer, as daylight fades more quickly, as plants and flowers disappear and the earth becomes bare, as the trees lose their leaves and we are left with the stark skeletons of their forms against the sky, we have this yearly reminder of loss, of darkness, of death. And yet simultaneously we know that it will not last for ever – that it is only the necessary precursor of growth.

※

Lent, in our northern hemisphere falling in spring, reminds us that the grain of wheat must fall and die, and we see how the ground has to be harrowed before the seed can take root. That harrowing has two senses. It means to break up the ground, to till the soil, turning it over and over until it becomes sufficiently broken up to receive the seed. But harrowing also means pain, mental anguish. Our harrowing means that we too have to be turned up and over if the seed is to come to life in us. We also have to let the husk fall away. We have to let go of the outer shell which seemed such a safe shelter, which seemed to promise such protection. Harrowing involves opening up. We are being asked to shed the husk, to be shaken loose, open. For only then does growth into new life become possible.

❦

But coming to life, finding new life, does not happen automatically. I have a mental picture of the harrowing of hell. God is reaching down to Adam and Eve to pull them up out of the pit. They are clinging hard to his hand. This is vital. New life is being offered, not forced.

"Awake, O sleeper."

Those words from the homily for Holy Saturday have a dramatic quality.

> Awake, O sleeper, and arise from the dead, and Christ shall give you life. I am your God, who for your sake became your Son, who for you and your descendants now speak and command with authority those in prison, come forth, and those in darkness, have light, and those who sleep, rise.
>
> I command you, Awake sleeper. I have not made you to be held a prisoner in the underworld. Arise from the dead; I am the life of the dead. Arise O man, O woman, work of my

hands, arise, you who were fashioned in my image.

Here is the promise:

that I shall not be asleep but awake
that I shall not be in prison but be set free
that I shall not have darkness but light
that I shall have not death but life.

"Anyone is entitled to discover in the midst of their winter an unconquerable summer."

Who would have thought my shrivel'd heart
Could have recover'd greenness? It was gone
Quite underground; as flowers depart
To see their mother-root, when they have blown;
Where they together
All the hard weather,
Dead to the world, keep house unknown.

It is up to me to grasp what is being offered. I may hear and see the good news of the resurrection but until it engages my total attention I may well fail to *recognize* it.

So Mary stands at the tomb for a long time before she turns round to see who is there beside her.

So the disciples trudge along that road to Emmaus for a long time before they notice who has been with them for so much of the way.

After the resurrection Christ presents himself to each person in a way, and at a time and a place, appropriate to each. It is never a case of rejecting the ordinary (a lakeshore, a garden, a dusty road) but rather of penetrating through appearances, going beyond the familiar. For this new life is never anything remote or mysterious. It means being totally present in my everyday life. It is there and nowhere else that I will discover it. Christ has asked me to "die" so that I can really begin to live *now*. This is what the fourth gospel calls abundant life. It is a new and fuller life; it means not so much any external difference as a different quality of life.

I think that it means above all the avoidance of fantasy. I also suspect, though I really cannot be quite sure, that it is one of God's gifts to us as we grow older, that in the second half of our lives the paschal mystery touches us more closely. As our bodies become less strong, and our faculties begin to fail, we are forced to recognize what diminishment may mean, and we have to accept the many things that we will never do, the many doors now closed to us. This faces us with reality, no longer with day dreams and extravagant plans. There is less opportunity now to evade the real. It feels like a narrowing down of possibilities, and yet at the same time an invitation to go deeper into reality – perhaps less achieving for God and more receiving from God.

※

At every eucharist I see the bread broken, the wine poured out. That action also established the pattern by which I live my own life, day by day, and year by year. The very symbols of the eucharist hold a double message. They are ambiguous symbols. They confront me once again with paradox.

Bread speaks to me of life. Yet the breaking of that bread does not only mean sharing, it means the destruction that must preceed the sharing. The body broken in death makes possible the new life.

The wine is a symbol of rejoicing, the fruit of the vine enjoyed among friends. But it is also the cup of blood drained from the body, the blood that signifies death.

So here is a daily reminder of this paradox.

> The breaking, the pouring out,
> lead to new life.
>
> We lose our life to gain it.
>
> Dying and behold we live on.

Praying the Conflicts

Praying Psalms (handwritten marginalia)

The contradictions which I find within myself are the basis from which I approach God in prayer if that prayer is to be an honest expression of the complex person that I am. For there can be no pretence in prayer. I stand before God as I really am – or at least that is what I really want to do, though far too often it seems to me that I have been encouraged ever since my earliest days by well meaning guides (parents, church, confirmation classes, prayer manuals) to turn to God the smiling and pleasant side of myself. This is why praying the psalms is such an excellent way of reaching God with the whole of my humanity.

❋

St Benedict has himself clearly been shaped by the psalms, and the Rule quotes them constantly, more frequently than any other biblical source. He clearly wished that in his monastery the life of the community and the life of each individual should also be shaped and formed by them. So the psalms hold the central place in the daily saying of the offices, and the whole psalter is recited weekly, until the words of the psalms would inform the mind and penetrate the heart. Benedictines are people of the psalms. St Benedict assessed anyone entering the community by the way in which he knew and loved the psalter. And those words of the *suscipe*, which the novice says on taking the vows, come from Psalm 118, words which will establish the whole relationship of each individual before God: "Receive me O Lord as you have promised, and I shall live."

❧

The psalms allow me to face my inner conflicts. They allow me to shake my fist at God one moment, and the next to break out into spontaneous song. I am angry, but then I am grateful. I complain at the bitterness of my lot, and then I rejoice at the untold blessings which I receive. If I discover the fullness of my own humanity I also discover the many faces of God. If the story of the people of Israel and their struggle in holding on to the covenant is also my own story, the psalms leave me in no doubt, as to the difficulties involved in that relationship. That in itself is consoling. For here is a people who experience struggle and sacrifice, who know the light and the dark, hunger and thirst, who grumble and complain, and who rejoice and praise – and who have no inhibitions in doing this completely openly and vigorously.

❧

There is nothing hidden when I pray the psalms. "O Lord, all I long for is before you." When I say that I feel that I am talking to my creator who knows me better than I know myself. I stand before God with a sense of mystery in the face of the amazing miracle of my creation. "For you have created my inward parts; you knit me together in my mother's womb. You knew my soul and my bones were not hidden from you. Your eyes saw my limbs when they were yet imperfect, and in your book were all my members written" (Psalm 139: 12–15). This is the total openness, the laying aside of appearances, the taking off of the mask that the psalms make possible.

I present myself before the God who has called me by name because he loves me – and for no other reason.

> He knows me through and through from having watched my bones take shape in my mother's womb.

> He reads my thoughts, my feelings and my longings.

> He is concerned for me in my joys and in my frustrations, in my weakness and in my strength.

> He sees me in laughter and in tears, in illness and in health.

> He shares my memories of the past as well as my hopes and my expectations for the future.

As he listens to my breath and to my heart
beat he knows me better than I know myself.[1]

🝊

At the times when I feel ajar I can lay it all out before
him, every ache in my body, the sense of being torn
apart. "My heart is in tumult, my strength fails me,
and even the light of my eyes has gone from me . . .
my loins are filled with a burning pain and there is
no sound part in all my body." (Psalm 38:7, 9, 10).
Or again, "I am poured out like water and all my
bones are out of joint; my heart within my breast is
like melting wax. My mouth is dried up like a
potsherd; and my tongue clings to my gums." (Psalm
22:14–15). There is no pretence here. And then I
ask, "How long, O Lord, will you so utterly forget
me?" (Psalm 13:1). The psalms speak for me when
all my safe plans for my life disappear or all my inner
certainties dissolve. That vivid imagery of drowning
– and that is precisely what it feels like – becomes a
cry, "The waves have come up even to my throat.
The waters of death encompassed me; and the floods
of chaos overwhelmed me." (Psalm 18:4)

🝊

Often I turn to God in anger. I accuse him of being
grossly unfair, of inflicting on me suffering that I do
not deserve. "All this has come upon us though we
have not forgotten you; we have not betrayed your
covenant. Our hearts have not turned back nor have

our steps strayed from your paths . . . Rouse yourself, O Lord. Why do you sleep?" (Psalm 44:18, 23). What sort of a God is this? I hurl reproaches at him, not only for what is happening but for the callous way in which it seems that he is not prepared to do anything about it. "Why do you hold back your hand; why do you keep your right hand in your bosom?" Equally I feel no hesitation in expressing my anger towards those who have treated me so badly, or whom I feel are responsible for so much of my pain and suffering. I want them to suffer too. "Let them be disgraced and dismayed for ever; let them be confounded and perish" (Psalm 83:17). "Let them be like chaff before the wind; with the angel of the Lord driving them; let their way be dark and slippery; with the angel of the Lord pursuing" (Psalm 35:5, 6, 7). And when that psalm continues, "For without cause they have secretly spread a net for me; without cause they have dug a pit to entrap me." I find I am facing something which I might otherwise try to evade, and that it is in fact all my own inner bitter feelings and resentments in which I have become totally ensnared. And then I look at myself and my prayer becomes "O Lord my God, I cried to you: and you have made me whole." (Psalm 30:2)

※

The psalms allow me to present this very inchoate picture of myself to God. It is precisely this holding together of the differences that makes the psalms so rich and so real for me. There is no attempt to impose coherence. That is precisely one of their greatest strengths. Much of what is said comes over as disjointed exclamation, as ejaculatory expressions welling up out of my depths. There is no literary polishing which would try to tidy up all these feelings. So at one moment I am cast down and the next I am full of confidence in God's love and power. "God my joy and my delight" (Psalm 43:4), "My heart dances for joy" (Psalm 28:8). Here are the prayers of certainty. "Great is your abiding love toward me" (Psalm 86:13). And then I look beyond myself to the whole of creation. "The heavens are yours, so also is the earth: you founded the world and all that is in it" (Psalm 89:11). There are times when I can shout for joy at the vision of the world in which everything is in its proper place, nature and men and women and God. Grass for the cattle, the trees are watered, the sun knows the hour of its setting, and the moon keeps to its seasons – the litany goes on, and best of all is the fact that this keeps my own life span in its proper perspective. "Man goes out to his work; and to his labour until the evening" (Psalm 104:23).

❦

As I pray the psalms I am faced once again with the fact that I am solitary, and unique, and yet at the same time connected in my being to others. I see myself as part of the whole, I have a sense of solidarity both with the rest of the human race and with the universe itself. This for me is one of the most important aspects of the psalms. For they are at once intensely personal – they could have been written for me alone, so well do they serve my own individual need – and yet they are also completely universal, and I realize that for thousands of years they have been used by people just like me. So while I know that I am unique and that God in his love created me as I am, I have also to recognize that I share that humanity, that what is true for me is also true for others. This solidarity extends beyond the bounds of temporal time. It makes me one with the present but part of the past too. So when the psalms allow me to identify myself with the chosen people of Israel and their long and difficult search for God, I find my own past too.

The Israelites knew good times and bad times. Much was failure, sin, the refusal to listen, the inability to hear the voice of God. Perhaps I can see here something which tells me about my own life, and the presence of a God who speaks and waits for my response. This is of course simply that dialogue which St Benedict makes central to the Benedictine life, and of which there is the daily reminder in the words of Psalm 95: "*Today* if only you would hear his voice". That is an equally urgent reminder for me today, and every day. I need to listen, and to hear not what I want to find but in whatever way it is that God is trying to reach me. But, just as in any other relationship, I know how easy it is not to hear the other. God's letting go of me has given me that freedom to hear or not to hear, to respond or not. Here I am faced with a relationship with God which is asking me to be open to him in whatever way he chooses to reach me. This asks me to be vulnerable to his word minute by minute. If I am to live this way it prevents me from imposing any neat or safe pattern on my life. It forces me to live provisionally. It forces me to see that I must be prepared to live with the brokenness around me. I shall go on searching for healing and for wholeness, and at the same time I shall hold on to the possibility that this may not be part of God's plan. I have to recognize that the tensions I find within myself may not be resolved after all, and that perhaps I have to learn to live with the contradictions and try to see that at their heart lies the mystery of God, a God who is both certain and unpredictable, utterly safe and yet also surprisingly explosive.

ℜ

This is both disturbing and reassuring. Again I see the irony in having arrived at this point. For I find that instead of looking for either/or I can now hold on to both/and. This allows me to live with the muddle, the untidiness, the incomprehension. I no longer expect there to be some neat pattern in things, a wonderfully fulfilling coming together. Instead I am able to say that after all I don't know, and to find in saying that that I am saying something which is positive and liberating. For if I can see this then I can also see that in the end there is only mercy, the most perfect expression of God's love. I hold on to the promise of the Rule "Never to despair of God's mercy".

🙰

"Show us your mercy, O Lord: and grant me your salvation" (Psalm 85:7). "Be merciful to me, O Lord; for I call to you all the day long" (Psalm 86:3). "But when I said 'My foot has slipped' your mercy, O Lord, was holding me" (Psalm 94:18). Again and again this is the refrain. After I have experienced and expressed the whole range of my feelings this final confidence in God's mercy remains. This is the God who can turn the rock into a pool of water and the flint-stone into a springing well (Psalm 114:8) just when I could not believe that this could ever happen. This is also the God who will bring me to the foot of the Cross time and again. And this, though I find it hard to understand, is his greatest mercy. This is no easy way to follow. This is no facile promise that the way will not be rough and the going hard. Yet I also know that this is a God who loves me and will never let me go; and the paradox of that is that this is a God who loves me enough to let me go. I have to live with this as the ultimate contradiction: the God who lets me go is the God who holds me.

So once more I find myself praying those words of the *Suscipe*,

"O God in your mercy accept me, receive me, support me, uphold me", now today, tomorrow and for the rest of my life until the other side of the grave when at last all will be resolved and I shall see everything in the light of Easter and the glory of the risen Christ.

XII

Yes

In the Prologue to the Rule St Benedict presents us with that vivid image of the Lord standing in the marketplace calling out to the passers-by: "Is there anyone here who yearns for life and desires to see good days?"

If I say, "Yes, I do", and if I set out with St Benedict as my guide, I have no illusions about what is involved. He tells me that at first the way will be hard and narrow. He does not promise me escape from pain, rather "we shall through patience share in the sufferings of Christ". But he also describes this way as "the way of life". He promises that as we run and make progress our hearts will become "overflowing with the inexpressible delights of love", until at last we reach our heavenly home.

To say Yes to this invitation and set out with St Benedict is an extraordinary affirmation. Yes is a daring word, one that requires courage. To say Yes implies risk. It means moving forward. It reminds me of something that Dag Hammarsjköld says in *Markings*: "At some moment I did say Yes . . . and from that hour I was certain . . . that my life, in self-surrender, had a goal." This is the Yes to Christ's call to discipleship.

138

❧

It is not, and it never can be, a Yes said simply with the mind, an intellectual conviction. It has to be the Yes that comes from the heart, the Yes that I say with body, mind and spirit, the whole of my being. What this means is that I have to descend into the depths of myself, to the real self without the mask, the self that lets go of appearances, before I can say it. It comes from me alone, for it is my own unique and individual response to that invitation. That is why I often find it frightening. For it involves a huge act of faith, standing alone, admitting my total dependence. Yet at the same time I know it would never be possible unless I knew I was held up and supported by my brothers and sisters in Christ – the individual and the community held together in tension, something that we have all experienced.

❧

My Yes means that I try to listen to God in all the many ways that he speaks to me; that I hear and respond – so this is the Yes of obedience.

My Yes means that I accept the present and do not try to run away from myself, but remain where I am, firmly rooted and accepting myself – so this is the Yes of stability.

My Yes means that I live open to the new and that I am ready to journey on, to move forward whatever the cost – so this is the Yes of *conversatio morum*.

※

So it is a Yes to the continual certainty of God, and Yes to the continual unpredictability of God. It is Yes to a series of ever-opening doors. It is a Yes in which I know that I shall never escape the contradictions but throughout my life I shall go on struggling to hold them together. For this knowledge, at once reassuring and liberating, I am deeply grateful.

※

So it is also the Yes of continual gratefulness, the Yes of wonder and surprise at the never-ending generosity of a God who continually showers on me gifts of all kinds – even perhaps the gift of failure. I love the way in which William Law speaks of this:

If anyone would tell you the shortest, surest way to all happiness, all perfection, he would tell you to make a rule to yourself to thank and praise God for *everything* that happens to you. For it is certain that whatever seeming calamity happens to you, if you thank and praise God for it, you turn it into a blessing. Could you therefore work miracles, you could not do more for yourself than by the thankful spirit, for it heals with a word spoken, and turns all that it touches into happiness.

There is also this splendidly pithy saying from David Steindl-Rast:

We tend to think that the happy people are grateful because they got what they like. In reality the grateful people are happy because they like what they got.

❦

I pray Yes at the start of every day, accepting what lies ahead and hoping that I may, in all that happens, see and feel and know the presence of God.

I pray Yes at the end of every day as I hand all that has happened over to God and ask his blessing on it.

So that Yes that I say in prayer gradually becomes my Yes to the whole of life. The Yes that holds everything together; that brings everything into focus and gives it meaning.

> You dare your Yes – and experience a meaning.
> You repeat your Yes – and all things acquire a meaning.
> When everything has a meaning how can you live by anything but a Yes?

❦

A half-hearted Yes, a Yes hedged about with conditions, will not do. It is no good to count the cost, to play safe. It's no good being the person with the divided heart that the psalmist knows (Psalm 119:113). So long as I am torn apart by the wrong sort of tension, by those destructive forces of disintegration, in the grip of old hurts and wounds that still hold me back, unforgiven and life-denying, I cannot give my whole and full and clear Yes – because I am still held in bondage to the past, and not yet free to move on into the future. Which is why daily forgiveness and the renewing of the covenant is a constitutive part of the life to which St Benedict points us.

꙰

The truth of my Yes only has its true meaning beyond success or failure. It only makes sense in the context of the pashcal mystery. My Yes points me to the folly of the Cross – or is it the wisdom of the Cross? It points me to that ultimate paradox: the failure that is a victory, to what the world would call utter foolishness, where losing is gaining, and where dying makes new life possible. A paradox which all of us know in our hearts is true. For there is not one of us who has not had some dying to do, some painful death to go through – and who also has not found that miracle, that from death comes life.

꙰

Nor is it enough to say Yes just once. I have to say it time and again, to repeat it and go on repeating it. Sometimes I find it difficult, almost impossible to say. I feel that I am like Jacob wrestling through the night, and sometimes it feels like a very long night. And perhaps it goes on so long because like Jacob I have not recognized with whom I am wrestling. I have still not learnt to recognize God in his many guises: I have been made blind and deaf by my own concerns and needs and anxieties, by my pride, by my desire for security. But when I give up wrestling with God I can look around me and say like Jacob, "Truly, the Lord was in this place and I knew it not" (Genesis 28:16).

Like Mary at the tomb I turn round and I find Christ there.

This is the greatest Yes of them all.

In saying it I join with Christ's own Yes. "The son of God, Christ Jesus . . . was never a blend of Yes and No. With him it was, and is, Yes. For all the promises of God find their Yes in him." (2 Corinthians 1:19,20).

In Christ all things will be well.

In Christ all things will be brought together – all those tensions and contradictions, brought together in a man who was so at one with himself that he sleeps in the boat while the storm rages around him.

It is only in and through him, in and through that amazing, total, first and unconditional love, that I can say my Yes.

And so I join my Yes with that of Mary, a fiat, a joyous fiat, Yes – let it be according to thy will.

And so I join my Yes with all those who down the ages have said *Suscipe me*, "Accept me, O Lord, receive me, support me, uphold me as you have promised and I shall live; do not disappoint me in my hope."

Notes and Comments

Explanation

The first 'Benedictine Experience' was held in Canterbury in the summer of 1983 under the auspices of the Canterbury Cathedral Trust in America, and I am extremely grateful to all those involved and in particular to Mr Sam Belk the chairman who helped to make that possible. The Rev. John Mitman who acted as chaplain in those early years also played an important role in establishing it. From this small beginning have grown a number of 'Benedictine Experiences' now held regularly in England and in America, some happening every year, others once only or for some special occasion. Just as in any traditional Benedictine community the ethos of each is quite distinct, determined by the place itself and the people who are part of it. So while California and mid-Wales, Chicago and Glastonbury will each follow a common pattern and rhythm they will also develop their own particular character, an expression of that unity and diversity found within the Benedictine tradition.

Prologue

The Prologue is from *RB 1980, The Rule of St Benedict in English*, ed, Timothy Fry, O.S.B., the Liturgical

Press, Collegeville, Minnesota 1982, which is taken to be the definitive text. It is available simply in translation, or in an unabridged edition which also carries an introduction, commentary and notes: *RB 1980, The Rule of St Benedict in Latin and English with Notes*, ed. Timothy Fry, O.S.B., the Liturgical Press, Collegeville, Minnesota 1981. Another translation has been made by David Parry, O.S.B., Darton, Longman & Todd 1983.

Chapter 1

The short phrase I use on p. 12 comes from the *Life of Dunstan* by the anonymous clerk "B", and is quoted in its context in Douglas Dales, *Dunstan, Saint and Statesman*, Lutterworth Press, Cambridge 1988 p.30.

The reference to Jean Vanier is the first of many that I shall make throughout this book, for I find here a man who through his work with L'Arche, the communities he founded for the mentally handicapped, writes out of deep experience of our woundedness, our vulnerability, and our search for healing. This particular quotation is taken from *Man and Woman He Made Them*, Darton, Longman & Todd, London, and Paulist Press, New York 1985, p.61

I have always been greatly moved by those words in *Rule for a New Brother*, which I quote on page 18. There is now a new edition, with a foreword by Henri Nouwen, published by Darton, Longman & Todd, 1986 (see pp.3–4).

Those lines from a prayer of St Anselm are given in the translation by Sister Benedicta Ward, S.L.G.

The whole prayer may be found in *Prayers and Meditations of St Anselm*, Penguin, 1973, pp. 153–6.

Chapter 2

The description of St Benedict which opens this chapter comes from St Benedict of Aniane, in the preface to his early ninth-century *Concordia Regulorum*. Contemporary scholars debate which of St Benedict's sources prevail in the Rule. Adalbert de Vogue would say that it is the eremitical, Ambrose Wathen would say the coenebetic and communitarian. Thomas Keating, however, in an article in *Cistercian Studies*, 1976, XI, 4, 257–68, says that a case must be made for both. I found Michael Casey's article in *Trurunga*, 1985, 28, most useful in pointing out the implications of this text.

My thinking on the subject of paradox has been helped by three recent books. Parker Palmer, *The Promise of Paradox*, Ave Maria, 1980; Charles Elliott, *Praying through Paradox*, Fount, 1986; and Cyprian Smith, *The Way of Paradox, Spiritual Life as taught by Meister Eckhart*, Darton, Longman & Todd, 1987. The sentence quoted on p. 24 is from *Praying through Paradox*, p. 44. The paragraph quoted on pp. 24–5 is from *The Promise of Paradox*, p. 46, which I have found one of the most illuminating studies on this subject.

The biblical references are 2 Corinthians 12:10 and Matthew 10:39.

Maria Boulding says this in *Gateway to Hope, An Exploration of Failure*, Fount, 1985.

Chapter 4

The quotation on pp. 42–3 is from Bede Thomas Mudge, O.H.C., writing in the newsletter of the Order of Holy Cross, West Park, New York, for the autumn of 1986.

I cannot now remember where I read that sentence from Kathleen Raine.

The Celtic material is taken from the *Carmina Gadelica*, prayers and blessings from the Outer Hebrides which were collected and translated by Alexander Carmichael at the end of the last century. The most accessible anthology is now the selection that I edited, *The Celtic Vision*, Darton, Longman & Todd, London 1988.

Peter Van Breemen was writing in *As Bread that is Broken*, Dimensions, New Jersey 1974, p.10.

W. Paul Jones kept a diary of his time at Snowmass, the Trappist abbey in the Rockies, and it is published as *The Province Beyond the River. The Diary of a Protestant at a Trappist Monastery*, Paulist Press, New York 1981. The passage to which I refer comes on p.102.

The quotation on p. 49 is from a recent book by Henri Nouwen, *Lifesigns: Intimacy, Fecundity, Ecstasy in Christian Perspective*, Doubleday, 1986, p.63.

Chapter 5

I found Dame Janet Baker's declaration about herself very moving, which is why I use it to open this meditation. She was talking to the Rev. John Barton, and the interview was published in the

Fairacres Chronicle, S.L.G. Press, Oxford, Summer 1985 (Vol. 18, No 2) pp.18–29.

The American Benedictine Prioresses have issued a number of statements which are challenging declarations of what the Rule of St Benedict means for the world today. This and the statement on stewardship which I use in meditation VI are well worth seeing. They are available from the Benet Press, Erie, Pennsylvania, U.S.A.

Chapter 69 of the Rule is a rather mysterious chapter and lends itself to various interpretations. What I say here owes much to Brother Andrew Marr, O.S.B., an Anglican Benedictine at St Gregory's Abbey, in Three Rivers, Michigan.

The piece about Jean Vanier comes from Henri Nouwen's *Lifesigns*, p.34, and the later sentence is from the same book, p.71.

What I say about forgiveness in the Rule owes much to an article by Terence Kardong, "Repressed Anger in RB", *Trurunga*, 1980/2, pp.5–7.

The sentence on p. 64 is from Maria Boulding, *Gateway to Hope. An Exploration of Failure*, Fount, London 1985, p.19 cf. Micah 7:19.

The C. Day Lewis lines come from "Walking Away", in *Selected Poems*, Penguin 1969, p.35.

The extract comes from a sermon by John Austin Baker preached in 1977 at the University Church of Christ the King, London.

Chapter 6

For these Celtic blessings see chapter IV.

The quotation comes from Donald Nicholl, *Holiness*, Darton, Longman & Todd, 2nd ed., 1987, p.29.

I was very struck by these words of Maria Boulding, O.S.B. when I first read them in an article in *The Times* in 1980, celebrating the quincentenary of the birth of St Benedict, which was showing his relevance for the world today. The sentence is taken from an equally arresting statement by the American Benedictine sisters of whom I wrote earlier in the notes to chapter V.

I do not think that I had seen the contrast between consecration and desecration ever put so dramatically as in this passage from Wendell Berry, *The Gift of Good Land*, North Point Press, San Francisco 1981, p.281.

John Howard Griffin's *The Hermitage Journals* remains one of my most favourite books, one that I return to time and again not only for what it tells me about Thomas Merton but for what Howard Griffin writes about solitude and silence and the contemplative view of the world. It is published by Andrews and McMeel, Kansas City and New York 1981, and this particular passage will be found on p.81.

The description of the hillside at Gethsemani, which I have included because I enjoy so much the lyrical quality of the writing and the vision of the world that it conveys, is from Matthew Kelty, *Sermons in a Monastery: Chapter Talks*, ed. William Paulsell, Cistercian Publications 1983, p.46.

The lines are from Alice Walker's amazing novel *The Color Purple*, Washington Press, New York 1983, pp.176 and 178.

I am not sure now where the phrase I quote on page 79 Brother David Steindl-Rast's occurs. But this is really more or less the whole theme of that lovely book *Gratefulness, Prayer of the Heart, An Approach to Life in Fullness*, Paulist Press 1984.

Walter Brueggeman, American Protestant theologian, has much that is exciting to say, particularly when he writes about the psalms. That small phrase of his I can no longer trace, but it is very typical of so much that he is saying.

Chapter 7

Henri Nouwen's account of his time at Genesee remains, I think, one of the best introductions to what the monastic life is all about, not least because it includes the conferences given by the abbot John Eudes Bamberger. *The Genesee Diary. Report from a Trappist Monastery*, Doubleday 1981, p.48.

On page 86 I am quoting something found in Matthew Kelty's *Sermons in a Monastery*, which I used in the previous chapter. These particular lines come from p.64.

This quotation is from a paper on "Individual and Community" given by Father Dominic Milroy, O.S.B. to the headmasters' conference.

I end this section with something that I read in David Steindl-Rast *A Listening Heart. The Art of Contemplative Living*, Crossroad, New York 1983, p.24.

The lines are from Khalil Gibran, *The Prophet*, pp.16–17.

I first read Anne Morrow Lindbergh many years

ago and had quite forgotten it. I was therefore delighted to find her book re-issued in a new edition, and that it still spoke to me as immediately today as when I had first read it. *Gift from the Sea*, new edition with an Afterword by the author, The Hogarth Press, London 1985; the quotations come from pp.5 and 44.

I found the Alexander Schmemann story in Alan Jones, *Soul Making; Desert Way of Spirituality*, SCM Press, 1986.

Perhaps what I am trying to say at the end of this meditation is best caught in that familiar but still deeply moving passage by Merton from *Conjectures of a Guilty Bystander*, Garden City, NY, Doubleday, 1966 p. 156ff. "In Louisville, at the corner of Fourth and Walnut, in the center of the shopping district, I was suddenly overwhelmed with the realization that I loved all those people, that they were mine and I theirs, that we could not be alien to one another even though we were total strangers. It was like walking from a dream of separateness." We each belong to one another.This is the spirituality of co-inherence which Merton himself expressed both in his writing and in his life.

Chapter 8

What I say on page 93 about "self-surrender" is taken from Thelma Hall, *Too Deep for Words, Rediscovering Lectio Divina*, Paulist Press, 1988, p.23.

I use Peter Van Breemen again as I always find his

way of expressing things so vivid and fresh. This particular quotation comes from p.41.

That phrase "Humility is facing the truth" comes in fact from an article by Cardinal Basil Hume, "The Monastic Ideal in Earthenware Vessels", *American Benedictine Review*, March 1981, 32:1, 6–7.

In writing about chapter 7 of the Rule, Father Daniel Rees used those two short phrases on p. 97 in *Consider Your Call. A Theology of the monastic life today*, ed. Daniel Ress, S.P.C.K. 1980, p.101.

The English Benedictine is Alan Rees, writing in *Touch of God, Eight Monastic Journeys*, ed. Maria Boulding, S.P.C.K. 1982, p.57.

Chapter 9

The quotation on page 100 comes from an article by David Steindl-Rast, "Man of Prayer", in *Thomas Merton, A Monastic Tribute*, ed. Patrick Hart, Cisterican Studies, Kalamazoo 1974, p.84.

I found the ideas that I refer to on pages 104–5 in David Steindl-Rast, *Listening Heart*, p.34, and in Basil Hume, *Searching for God*, Hodder & Stoughton, 1983, pp.32–4. But I have kept no note of where I found what I quote from Mother Teresa.

The Merton image of the spring and the stream I owe to Thelma Hall, *Too Deep for Words*, Paulist Press, 1988, p.11.

This small phrase at the bottom of page 105 is taken from the American Benedictine sisters' statement on stewardship, which I have used so frequently because I find it one of the clearest expressions of what is implied in applying the Rule to daily living.

Archbishop Rembert Weakland has a most interesting discussion, which I refer to briefly, in the *American Benedictine Review*, March 1981, 23:1, pp.46ff. The image of the wheel, which I use on page 109, is also taken from this same article; it comes from Cardinal Pironio's introduction to the Rule in Spanish.

The quotation from Thomas Merton on pp. 107–8 is from something that can be found in an article, "Inner experience, Prospects and Conclusions", *Cistercian Studies*, 1984, 4, pp.336ff.

The phrase "interior openness to the world" is taken from something written by Aquinara Bockmann, in the *American Benedictine Review*, 1986, 37, p.304.

Chapter 10

The small phrase on pp. 116–7 is taken from a book that I have used before, Maria Boulding, *Gateway to Hope. An Exploration of Failure*, Fount, 1985, p.90.

I have also used the *Hermitage Journals* before (see the reference in Notes and Comments to chapter VI).

The quotation is from Peter Van Breemen's *As Bread that Is Broken*, p.140.

What I say about the feast of John the Baptist was inspired by Matthew Kelty in *Flute Solo, Reflections of a Trappist Hermit*, Doubleday, 1980, p.50.

That short Zen-like sentence on p. 125 is in fact a

quotation from Camus which comes to us by way of a Zen book. It was used by Monica Furlong in an article in *The Tablet*, 20th June 1987, and caught my imagination when I read it. The familiar but still perennial lines from George Herbert are from "The Flower", *The Temple, Sacred Poems and Private Ejaculations*, 1633. The edition I used was *George Herbert, The Country Parson, The Temple*, ed. John N. Wall, Classics of Western Spirituality, S.P.C.K., London 1981, p.291.

What I say here about the resurrection owes much to something I read in Michael Marshall, *A Change of Heart, A Spirituality of Encounter and Intimacy*, Collins, 1987, pp.119 and 28.

Chapter 11

I must acknowledge a debt to Peter Van Breemen, *op. cit.*, p.48, who gave me the idea of adapting Psalm 139 in this way.

The quotations from the psalms in this meditation are taken from the Alternative Semica Book and all references therefore follow the Hebrew numbering.

Chapter 12

The quotation, which I expect will be familiar to many, is from Dag Hammarskjöld, *Markings*, translated from the Swedish by Leif Sjöberg and W. H. Auden, Knopf, Penguin, London and New York 1964, p.110.